Managing Chaos

Managing Chaos

Dynamic Business Strategies in an Unpredictable World

Ralph D Stacey

KOGAN
PAGE

First published in 1992
Reprinted 1992, 1993, 1995

Kogan Page Limited
120 Pentonville Road
London N1 9JN

© Ralph D Stacey 1992

HD
58
.9
S72

British Library Cataloguing in Publication Data

A CIP record for this book is available from the British Library.

ISBN 0 7494 0681 X

Typeset by Saxon Printing Ltd, Derby
Printed and bound in Great Britain by
Biddles Ltd, Guildford and King's Lynn

Contents

Preface

You are only going to survive the increasing onslaughts of international competition in the business world these days if your organisation is creative; if it can generate new strategic directions faster than your rivals. That's the cliché we all repeat! But what we in the business community of the Western world have not yet come to grips with is this: the very way we focus on that task of creativity makes it pretty likely that we are going to continue retreating before the advancing Far East. Let me explain.

The great majority of Western managers now focus through a strongly shared dominant mindset on their primary task of creativity. I call that focus the paradigm of the stable equilibrium organisation: the belief that long-term success flows from stability, harmony, regularity, discipline and consensus. This mindset leads managers to demand general prescriptions they can immediately turn into successful action. The mindset determines what kind of prescriptions they will hear and act upon. The most immediately acceptable prescriptions are to: formulate visions; prepare long-term plans; set strategic milestones and monitor achievements against them; set out mission statements and persuade people to share the same culture; encourage widespread participation and consensus decision making; install control systems so that top executives can set the direction and stay in control.

Few ever question the mindset that leads to these prescriptions and to the enthusiasm with which they are received. Why should they question? After all, the stable equilibrium organisation paradigm is consistent with our scientific education and it is reinforced by the management textbooks and development programs. It is a clear message: you either install stability and achieve success or you experience instability and thus failure.

The problem is that this fundamental belief, so regularly reinforced by mainstream management writings, is simply wrong. This matters greatly because it leads Western managers through a preoccupation with laying off and spreading risks to strategies of repetition and imitation. In fact, success does not flow from choices between stability and instability; it emerges from choices of both stability and instability. When you think in this more sophisticated way you will not be confined to repetition and imitation. Why should we reach these conclusions?

First, the 'either/or' view is no longer a sustainable scientific point of view when it comes to understanding complex systems. We now know that nature's systems are continually creative because they are driven by stable laws that generate specific instability within recognisable patterns. Nature positively uses contained instability to generate variety and develop new directions. In nature, success is related to both stability and instability. This book will persuade you that the same point applies to successful businesses, giving you a new perspective that will change the way you design your actions. Such change is necessary because, as we are becoming increasingly aware, our Western tendency to see things in 'either/or' terms puts us at a disadvantage compared to the Eastern mind that is culturally more comfortable with paradox, with 'and/both' choices.

Future success will therefore begin in our minds, with our ability to change the way we focus on the world of business. I will argue that we are in great need of a new frame of reference: the paradigm of the far-from-equilibrium organisation. When we focus on the world with this new mindset, we will see that creativity is intimately connected with instability, with tension, conflict and the changing perspectives this provokes.

If you stick to the old stable equilibrium way of seeing your organisational world, you will simply repeat your past or imitate others who are already moving on to better things. If you lower that preoccupation with stability, that primitive defence against anxiety, you will open up the potential for creativity. But there is a price to pay – you will have to accept that the future direction of your organisation is unknowable. This means that no one can be in control of that future direction because unknowable directions emerge from the spontaneous, self-organising interaction between people. Those directions are exciting but unpredictable voyages of discovery, not safe package holidays.

It is the purpose of this book to explore what the new far-from-equilibrium paradigm means and what difference the change of focus makes to the actions that managers must design to achieve success. The re-focus has profound consequences for the entire approach we adopt to the strategic management of a business.

This book is addressed to all managers who believe that their organisation will not survive unless its capability for change and creativity is dramatically enhanced.

Chapter 1 explains the viewpoint that has been so baldly stated in this Preface.

Chapter 2 sets out what today's dominant mindset is, how it leads to certain kinds of prescriptions that are not working, and why managers need to change it.

Chapter 3 introduces the new paradigm. It explains what a far-from-equilibrium organisation is and why it is that even the best organisations seem periodically to fail. The chapter builds that explanation on the discoveries mathematicians and scientists have made about the chaotic and self-organising behaviour of complex feedback systems. This is the new scientific theory of management.

Chapter 4 focuses on the self-organising properties of complex systems, reviving the ancient idea that creativity and destruction are intimately connected. It shows how new strategic directions emerge from unstable, but potentially creative political, learning and group processes.

Chapter 5 deals with strategic thinking. Most people believe that strategic thinking is simply the stretching of step-by-step analytical logic over long time periods. In fact strategic thinking is dramatically different to this. It is the activity of seeing patterns rather than specific cause and effect links. It is rearranging paradoxes using analogies and intuition, all provoked by conflict and dialogue with others.

Chapter 6 explains why new strategic directions cannot be the realisation of the long-term intentions of top executives. Creative strategies can only emerge from the political interaction and group learning activities of people in an organisation. Long-term plans are simply rational defences against anxiety and visions are their mystical equivalent.

Chapter 7 explores how it is possible for behaviour in an organisation to be controlled even when no one can be in control of it.

Chapter 8 proposes that widespread participation in decision making is not an effective way for an organisation to cope with great uncertainty.

Chapter 9 sets out some very broad steps that could increase the capability of an organisation to learn, to create and thus to evolve. But this is not a book with lists of specific prescriptions for immediate action. Indeed it explains why the very idea that there can be a set of specific prescriptions for strategic management is an illusion.

Creative success lies in the reflective pause between a stimulus and the response to it. This book aims to be a reflective pause for action driven managers.

Ralph D Stacey
London
January 1992

1

Introduction to Managing Chaos

The aim of 'Managing Chaos' is to change the way managers think about the route to business success.

Today's dominant mindset leads managers to think that they must find the right kind of map before they embark upon the business journey into the future: you need to know where you are going and have some notion of how to get there before you set out, is the 'common sense' belief. The problem, however, is that the great majority of managers in the Western world are using the same standard maps to travel along transparent routes, leaving them wide open to the attacks of more imaginative competitors from the Far East. And those standard old maps are full of mythical routes that have outlived their usefulness. Indeed the very idea that a map can be drawn in advance of an innovative journey through turbulent times is itself a fantasy.

When they think in the alternative way which is to be explained in this book, innovative managers know that it is impossible to establish where they are going, or how they are going to get there, before they embark on the journey. It is through the journeying itself that a route and a destination are discovered: you have continually to make new maps as you travel if you wish to discover new lands. The key to success lies in the creative activity of making new maps, not in the imitative refining and following of already existing ones.

And this shift in perspective brings with it major changes in the way managers act. Let me explain.

THE OLD MAP THAT GUIDES MANAGERS TODAY – THE ROUTE TO STABLE EQUILIBRIUM ORGANISATIONS

It is rare indeed for Western managers to question the fundamental navigational principles they almost all use to find the route through ambiguous and highly uncertain situations to the land of long-term business success.

The first of these navigational principles has to do with the visionary Chief Executive Officer and the cohesive management team. Like the captain of a ship in troubled waters, top executives are supposed to locate the future destination of the ship and guide it to that point. Effective top executives are in control of the organisation and its journey because of the systems of rules and regulations they have installed and the long term plans they have devised – they tack and trim to keep the organisation on course; or when absolutely necessary they give the instruction for a change in direction.

The second navigational principle is the common culture. Managers and staff throughout the organisation are supposed to share the vision and believe in the same mission or business philosophy. They must 'all pull together' and 'sing off the same hymn sheet'. All must follow the rules, one of the most important of which is to check out the impact on the bottom line before doing anything. What is the rate of return? What is the level of risk? These are the key questions.

The third principle is about delivering what the customer wants. The organisation is supposed to identify what its customers want and then deliver it, so adapting more closely to the environment than its competitors do: the ship must move with the winds and the tides if it is to get anywhere.

Combine these three principles in a consistent, balanced manner and you will trace out today's dominant map of the route to success. That route is one that takes a firm to a state of stable equilibrium characterised by harmony, discipline, regularity and predictability. And this is such a comforting idea because it is about being 'in control', avoiding surprises, knowing where you are going, laying off risks and damping out differences. The stable equilibrium organisation reduces anxiety levels for everyone concerned.

You can observe the kind of behaviour this mindset leads to in just about every company in the UK and the USA. You can read about such behaviour in the newspapers every day. Let me give you an example taken from an article on the Technology page of the London *Financial Times* on 19 December 1991.

This particular article is headed 'Shareholders seek to bring R&D spending to account'. The article reports on a move to get companies to publish better information on their R&D efforts. The purpose of this is to enable institutional shareholders actively to exercise their responsibilities as owners. The idea seems to be that shareholders should be exercising more control and seeing to it that companies spend more on R&D. The purpose of publishing more information on R&D expenditure is also to enable shareholders to take a long-term view in valuing companies.

To achieve these purposes it is proposed that companies should: provide details on their strategy, including an indication of whether there is enough R&D expenditure to support the strategy; publish five year reviews of R&D expenditure, including product development; describe R&D work in progress; estimate likely rates of return on the expenditure and indicate risk levels; and explain how R&D expenditure translates into shareholder value. Shareholders should use official league tables on R&D expenditure as a basis for enquiring into low levels of expenditure.

This is what the Institutional Shareholders Committee, supported by the Bank of England, and the Department of Trade and Industry is pushing for. Bodies such as the Electronics Equipment Association are resisting it and the only reason they give for doing so is that there would be too great a disclosure of information to competitors. Nobody seems to be asking whether any of these proposals make sense in the first place; whether there is the remotest possibility that useful information of this kind could be provided; whether all this control over levels of expenditure actually leads to innovation.

Note the common concern with knowing what is going to happen, with being in control of innovation, with the stability all this implies. Since successful organisations are thought to be following the vision of their chief executives, none of these things should present any problems. Note the unquestioned assumptions that it is possible to know enough about what is going to happen to calculate meaningful future rates of return and levels of risk. Note how all parties to the policy debate simply accept the assumptions. Note the concern with top down intervention in the processes of innovation, with rules and regulations. Note the shared culture in which the bottom line is pre-eminent. All taking part in this debate are following the old map, with its routes to stable equilibrium, in the comfortable conviction that it is right. But is it?

THE NEW APPROACH – MAP-MAKING FOR SUCCESS AND FAR-FROM-EQUILIBRIUM ORGANISATIONS

The trouble with the standard maps and traditional navigational principles is that they can only be used to identify the routes that others have travelled before: they can only make sense when managing the knowable. Only then can the captain of the ship locate its destination. Only then does it make sense for the members of the team to follow the leaders slavishly. Only then can managers have the remotest idea of the future returns on R&D expenditure. But the old map is of little use at all when it becomes necessary to go where none have gone before. The old map helps little when it comes to that significant part of the real management problem: managing the truly unknowable. Small wonder then that cohesive management teams and visionary leaders are about as rare as mythical unicorns. Let me demonstrate what I mean.

Every practising manager knows from experience that the long-term future is unpredictable and full of surprises. By definition, innovative new strategic directions take an organisation where none has been before. It follows that no one can know the future destination of an organisation facing an unknowable future – instead managers have to discover and create it. If no one can know where the organisation is going then no one can be 'in control' – instead managers have to create conditions in which behaviour in an organisation is controlled although no one actually controls it. If managers cannot know where the organisation is going or what the right business philosophy for the future is, then they should not all believe in the same things – instead they should question everything and generate new perspectives through contention and conflict. And successful managers, partially creating and inventing their own environments, are doing much more than simply adapting. What managers are doing here is developing the navigational principles, drawing the maps, as they go along. This is what you have to do if you wish to go where none have gone before.

Conclude

To ground these points in management practice, consider the article which sits on the technology page of the *Financial Times* right next to the one discussed above on R&D expenditure. The heading is: 'Sony scattergun hits the target'.

The target in question is success for Sony's latest consumer electronics product innovation – the Data Discman. The Discman is a machine that weighs 500g and sits easily in the palm of your hand. Into the machine you load a compact disc containing dictionaries, books, language lessons, travel guides, quiz games and many more kinds of information. A liquid crystal display then provides you with pictures and accompanying these is CD quality speech and music. The Discman's dictionaries and language lessons pronounce the words and sentences in the voice of a native speaker – an invaluable aid to learning a new language. Before too long the Discman will enable you to carry a library around in your pocket and access passages from many books within seconds.

Sony is now churning out 20,000 of these personal information systems every month in Japan. In November 1991 it launched the product in Germany and the USA. The product will be launched in the UK, France and Spain in the Spring of 1992.

How did Sony develop this product? In 1988, a Sony employee, Yoshitaka Ukita, had to accept the failure of the 8cm single compact disc player which he was responsible for developing. However, he did not just give up: he tried to think of an alternative use for the failure. That was when he hit upon the idea of a personal information system. Ukita built enough support among his colleagues for taking the idea further. They approached publishers to put material on disc and software writers to prepare the programmes for organising and retrieving data. They began to reshape the distribution system so that both book stores and electronics shops would sell the product.

All this time the product was kept a secret even within Sony. But as the product launch date of 1 January 1990 approached, it became necessary to inform Norio Ohga, the Chief Executive of Sony. He made a design modification which delayed the product launch by six months, but he backed the idea. At first they expected to sell 5,000 units per month. Instead they sold 8,000 and now they are producing 20,000 per month. Ukita expressed his surprise at this outcome and he and his colleagues agree that no one knows how the product will develop from here.

Note how the executives at the top of the company were not in control of developing the product – they only heard about it when it was ready for launching. But the behaviour of Ukita and his colleagues was itself controlled – it had a self organising quality. Note how those involved got the forecasts wrong – they simply had no idea if the product would succeed or how well it might sell. They openly admit that they do not know what the future holds for the product now. Note how the product offering is shaping customer requirements – Sony does not simply adapt to its environment. Remember it keeps creating customer requirements through trial and error – the Walkman and the camcorder are other prominent examples of successful creation and Betamax is a well known example of failure. Note how the new product emerged from failure, from trial and error. It was not the realisation of a vision or some grand design. There was no map to follow before Ukita and his colleagues embarked on the journey: they made the map as they went along.

Examples such as this make it clear just how absurd it is to ask companies to publish information on the rates of return, the risk levels and the shareholder value their R&D expenditure is going to create. No one can possibly know these things if the R&D is going in anything like an innovative direction. Those who ask for this kind of information are driving according to the old maps. Those who innovate are making maps as they go.

Facing the unknowable

We are all aware that innovative futures are unknowable. But those using the old maps and navigational principles back away from this uncomfortable prospect by assuming that innovative futures are approximately knowable – you can at least have a vision or make some assumptions about the long-term future, so the proponents of the old approach say. It is possible, they think, to give shareholders, or someone else in a controlling position, meaningful information on future rates of return and risk levels. In so doing they are sustaining myths that protect them from having to face the anxiety provoked by the unknowable. And the trouble with comfortable fantasy worlds is that they distract attention from, and weaken the resolve to deal with, the real one.

This book is about facing unknowability head-on instead of sidestepping the issue by pretending that it is approximately known. The result is a new approach to managing that is far from comforting but far more dynamic and far more useful in turbulent times. It is an approach that has to do with creating the conditions in which the Ukitas of the West can self organise to innovate.

The new approach is disturbing because it means accepting that you really have no idea what the long-term future holds for your organisation; that you cannot be in control although the organisation itself can develop in a controlled manner in the right conditions; that it is harmful to secure uniformity by damping out differences between people.

The new approach is about sustaining contradictory positions and behaviour in an organisation: Sony has budgets and production schedules as well as hierarchies with power concentrated at the top, but it also enables individuals and groups to pursue new ideas in relative freedom.

The new approach is about positively using instability and crisis to generate new perspectives, provoking continual questioning and organisational learning through which unknowable futures can be created and discovered. For Ukita, the failure of the 8cm CD player was a crisis, but one from which he and those around him learned. Organisations such as Sony, which allow people to go so far down the road of developing a product before the top is involved, are bound to exhibit instability. And such instability is not an unfortunate, unintended consequence of innovation. Some Japanese companies purposely provoke instability: Honda hires large groups of managers in mid career from other organisations intentionally to create countercultures. Honda encouraged contention.

The new approach faces reality and accepts the consequent increase in levels of anxiety as necessary for creative activity. The stable equilibrium mindset is a defence against anxiety, one which blocks creative work. Unlike the stable equilibrium organisation destined to repeat its past, the far-from-equilibrium organisation is capable of an exciting, but unpredictable new journey. This is the kind of mindset managers need to cope with the unknowable future of innovative organisations.

But of course not all is unknowable. Probably most managers' jobs are dominated by the knowable – they usually know what outcome they need to achieve; the puzzle is how to do it. This is the case with the day-to-day management of the existing business. For this kind of normal puzzle-solving management, where the basic framework is given and constant, it is vital to use quantitative analysis to identify solutions to problems and apply systematic, formalised planning methods of implementation and control. Here, in relation to the short-term management of the existing business, the old mindset provides the essential guidelines.

But at the same time in different parts of the organisation, and at different times by the same people, it is necessary to practice frame-breaking extraordinary management, where managers conflict, question, learn and discover the new.

This is, perhaps, the chief contradiction of all – the structures and behaviour appropriate for stable normal management have to coexist with the informality and instability of extraordinary management which is necessary to cope with the unknowable. This contradiction places great tension on successful organisations, but that in itself can be the creative source of the company's continual development.

WHY IS A NEW APPROACH FOR MANAGING NECESSARY?

There are two sets of reasons why we need a new approach for managing:

1. The old approach is not serving the world of business very well.

2. The old approach is based on rarely questioned assumptions about the nature of systems that modern scientific discoveries show to be invalid.

THE SHORT LIVES OF ORGANISATIONS

Take the first reason. In 1983, Shell conducted a survey of how long business organisations survive.[1] This revealed that corporations live about half as long as individual human beings. The chances are that your organisation will die before you do.

This matters because it is a waste of resources and a substantial disruption to people's lives when organisations fail and new ones have to be set up. It also slows down the learning process about organising if we frequently have to go back to square one, starting with a small organisation and all its associated growing pains.

Look at the *Financial Times* Top 100 or the Fortune 500 over any recent five year period – the listings change dramatically. Think about the Peters and Waterman[2] sample of excellent companies – within five years of identifying them two-thirds slipped from the list. The simple truth is that we do not know how to sustain or replicate long-lived organisations.

And it is becoming clearer why organisations do not last all that long. Increasingly, recent studies make the point that managing by existing maps leads to imitation, repetition and excess.[3] When they manage continually with the stable equilibrium organisation recipe, managers seek to build on their organisation's existing strengths. They 'stick to the knitting' and steadily improve what they already do well. Then some more imaginative competitors come along and change the rules of the game. What was the source of competitive success becomes the reason for failure because the over-adapted company simply cannot change fast enough.

Take Texas Instruments (TI) as an example. It built its success on the ability to engineer cost reductions at a far faster pace than its rivals. It set the industry standards for semiconductors and produced an innovative flow of consumer products. But the attention to cost became an obsession. TI chased economies by offering customers cheaper and cheaper, but shoddier and shoddier outdated products. It was slow to move into the more sophisticated chips, leaving those lucrative areas for its rivals. TI was selling on the basis of price alone and ignoring the need to update its products. The source of its success became the reason for TI's decline. It was following the old map, building on its strengths, moving towards stable equilibrium.[4]

The old maps work for the normal day-to-day management of the existing business, but on their own they fail when it comes to continually developing the business. And those old maps fail because they simply reinforce the existing momentum of the business, leading to their strategic drift and eventual crisis from which they may or may not emerge successfully. The reality is *not* the stable equilibrium organisation: continuing success lies far-from-equilibrium.

THE INCONSISTENT BEHAVIOUR OF MANAGERS

The old approach also leads managers to do some pretty strange things. They say that success requires cohesive teams that share a vision and a culture, that pursue a strategic intent in a rational, orderly manner leading to adaptation to the market. Because they believe this, the Institutional Shareholders Committee in the example we discussed earlier is trying to get firms to disclose their rational, orderly strategies for innovation. Having made the firm's future knowable, it can then, presumably, be subjected to rational critique.

But when they stop avoiding the unknowable and actually confront strategic issues, by definition ambiguous and ill structured, managers usually split into conflicting factions around different intentions. Strategic choices then actually depend on how individual managers jostle and interact with each other in groups; on the kinds of political games they play and the organisational defence routines they employ. Action follows, sometimes after long delays, only if the group dynamics make group work possible and only when political support has been built to secure enough consensus. That action is usually experimental in nature and is often not centrally coordinated. Successful businesses do not just adapt, they create new markets. In practice, creative strategies emerge from instability in a seemingly unintended, uncoordinated manner. The way Sony actually developed the Discman bears this out.

However, although this is what actually happens, managers rarely discuss or examine the situation. Instead, they prepare plans which they find it impossible to implement because their world is changing so quickly. They do not analyse the functioning of their political system, that which actually determines what will happen.

How do managers get into this fix? I will argue in this book that the reason lies in the mindset that managers, and their consulting and academic advisors, bring to the task of strategic management. It seems that they are all unconsciously using long-term plans, team cohesion and organisational harmony as defences against the anxiety provoked by facing up to the unknowable. Unfortunately, the price of relief from anxiety is the loss of creative ability.

QUESTIONABLE ASSUMPTIONS ABOUT THE DYNAMICS

The second reason for disquiet with today's dominant maps of business success is that these maps are based on highly questionable assumptions about the nature of organisational dynamics; that is, about the pattern of interaction between people within an organisation and across its boundaries and about the patterns of behaviour generated by this interaction over time. Today's approach sees the dynamics of success as regular and stable patterns of behaviour. This idea is built on the assumption that it is possible, in principle, to predict the behaviour of an organisation – if you could not predict it you could not secure regularity and stability; you would have surprises and crises instead. Such predictability is only possible if there are clear-cut connections between cause and effect in business systems, that is, if a given action leads to a known outcome in known circumstances.

It is because we have such beliefs about cause and effect that we think it sensible to talk about long-term goals, missions and visions. If we could not identify the actions that lead to the goals, if there was no straight line connection between an action and a goal, then it would be idle speculation to talk about the goals we are going to achieve. Because our thinking is conditioned in this way we always explain success as the realisation of someone's vision. So, Federal Express is a great market creating success because its founder, Fred Smith, had a vision of a new parcel delivery service. Honda is a great global success because it has a powerful strategic intent to build motor engine competence. When we see a successful organisational effect we look in a straight line for the direct cause in some individual's vision.

But systems analysts have been telling us for years that in organisations the links between cause and effect are complex, distant in time and space, and very difficult to detect.[5] These analysts have pointed to the unintended and counterintuitive results that complex organisations produce. But few practical people seem to have heard the message. They seem to prefer sustaining the anxiety reducing fantasy of straightforward connections between cause and effect that allow them to continue believing in long-term plans.

However, mathematicians and natural scientists have recently made discoveries which make it even harder to avoid facing up to the complex behaviour of organisational systems.

These scientists have shown that certain kinds of systems – referred to as nonlinear feedback systems – operate in a state of bounded instability far-from-equilibrium. Now this may sound like a mouthful of scientific gibberish that has nothing to do with hard-nosed business people. But this book will make it clear why an innovative business is just such a system and why this is a fact of immense importance to the strategic management of a business.

The dynamics of simple non-linear feedback systems are so complex that the links between cause and effect are lost in the detail of what happens – tiny changes escalate, leading to massive consequences; virtuous and vicious circles are generated. Consequently it is totally impossible to predict the specific long-term future of such a system – it is truly unknowable.

The Discman example discussed earlier makes this quite clear. At the end of 1987 when Ukita was developing the 8cm compact disc player, neither he nor anyone else in the world knew that it would lead to Sony launching a successful new personal information system only two years later. What caused the Discman was not a simple vision, but a complex intertwining of events and people.

But there *are* recognisable categories of this unpredictable behaviour. These are qualitative similarities, family resemblance type features, constant irregularities, which skilled humans can recognise and cope with through analogous reasoning and intuition.

The inspiration for developing the personal information system came to Ukita when he juxtaposed the failed 8cm CD player with a Filofax and an electronic personal organiser. He was reasoning by analogy, no doubt also influenced by the successful Walkman, or personal entertainment system. Ukita and colleagues were learning too. They had learned from the Betamax failure. There, weak links with film stockists had been one of the undoings of the product. Ukita and colleagues saw the similarity, the general qualitative pattern, and made sure that they formed links with publishers and bookstores.

The dynamics here are characterised by irregularity and instability. Systems of this kind develop over time by passing through periods of instability, crisis or chaos, and produce new directions and new forms of order spontaneously.[6] Once again the example of the Discman typifies all these points.

This book contends that successful business organisations are what scientists have called non-linear feedback systems.[7] Such systems fail when they are taken to positions of stable equilibrium; they fail in the sense that they are trapped into simply repeating their past. But such systems succeed, they are creative, when they are sustained far-from-equilibrium in states of bounded instability.[8] There are scientific reasons for a new approach to managing because the old one is based on assumptions about the dynamics of systems that we know now to be untrue. The old approach is based on the assumption that the dynamics of success are stability and regularity. The new approach understands that the dynamics of success are irregularity and bounded instability.

WHAT THE NEW MANAGEMENT APPROACH MEANS

Using the new far-from-equilibrium management mindset, managers will see the world of organisations in a very different way. As a result they will design their actions differently according to these propositions:

- The long-term future is unknowable. It cannot be predicted to any useful extent. This follows from what scientists have discovered about nonlinear feedback systems, of which a business organisation is one. The unpredictability flows from the very structure of the business system itself, not simply because the markets and the technology keep changing. And the practice of innovation, the unknowability of the outcome of Sony's 8cm CD player for example, demonstrates how true this is.

- Consequently some single, organisation-wide intention in the form of a shared vision of a future state must be a dangerous illusion. This is clear when you consider Fred Smith's vision for Federal Express which came to be known as Zapmail. This attempt to create an electronic mail delivery service failed because of competition from cheap fax machines. Following that vision cost Federal Express billions. The same applies to long-term plans to realise such visions.

- Instead, effective management focuses on ever-changing agendas of strategic issues. These agendas consist of multiple challenges, stretching aspirations and ambiguous issues. The challenges, aspirations and issues all arise out of ill-structured and conflicting changes occuring in the here and now but having long-term, widespread consequences. Such a vibrant agenda of issues means that the organisation does not hitch its future to any one development alone. From all this, it is only with hindsight that we can detect a 'vision' or describe a plan. Think how well this describes the continuing agenda of product developments, successes and failures at Sony.

- Strongly shared cultures block an organisation's ability to develop and handle live strategic issue agendas. But contradictory counter-cultures foster different perspectives and provoke the enquiry and complex learning necessary to handle strategic issue agendas. Take General Motors with its bureaucracy and strong culture which has led it to follow for decades the same strategy of covering the whole market with its standard product lines. Then compare this with Honda, which promotes countercultures and contention. The comparison indicates that counter-cultures foster different perspectives and provoke the inquiry and complex learning necessary to handle strategic issue agendas.

- Cohesive teams of managers operating in a state of consensus are what is required for normal problem-solving management. But spontaneous, self-organising learning groups of managers, tackling conflict, engaging in dialogue and publicly testing assertions are vital to the handling of strategic issues.

- Normal day-to-day management must rely on decision making as a logical, analytical process. But the extraordinary management required to bring to the surface strategic issues and handle them in innovative ways has to rely on decision making which is an exploratory, experimental process based on intuition and reasoning by analogy. We saw how the development of the Discman relied on these processes.

- That normal day-to-day control and development of the business is the monitoring of progress against plan milestones. Control here means constraint by rules, systems and rational argument. But the control and development of the business in the open-ended, unknowable long term is a political process where the constraints are provided by the need to build and sustain support. Here control is a self-policing, learning process. Ukita would never have got anywhere with his Discman idea if he had failed to build the support of his colleagues and obtain the backing of the chief executive. That was a political process. While the product was being developed there was no reporting against milestones – the top executives did not even know it was happening. But this did not mean that Ukita and his colleagues were out of control. As a group developing the product they controlled themselves: their processes of learning about the product and their practices of sustaining support amongst themselves for the product were a form of control.

- New strategic direction is not the realisation of prior intent. New strategic directions emerge spontaneously from the chaos of challenge and contradiction, through a process of real-time learning and political interaction. That is what is so wrong about the proposed rules on R&D expenditure disclosure already referred to. Trying to impose rules like this is a static approach that can only work for normal management, not the frame-breaking management that R&D should be.

- Top executives do not drive and control new strategic direction. Effective top executives create favourable conditions for, and participate in, complex learning and effective politics.

- Normal day-to-day management can be guided by general models and common prescriptions applicable to many different specific situations: following the old standard map. But innovation and new strategic direction require extraordinary frame-breaking management: the development of new mental models for each new strategic situation. This is a process of making a new map for each new strategic situation. It is important to stress this point because the old mindset has conditioned us to believe that there is a system we can install, a set of prescriptions we can establish, a prior map we can follow, to achieve success. With the new mindset we can see that no one, no book, can prescribe systems, rules, policies or methods that will lead to innovative success. All we can do is describe the conditions which appear to enable groups of people to learn what approaches are effective in each new situation, as they engage in it.

- Continuing success flows from non equilibrium, creative interaction with the environment, not adaptive equilibrium that simply comes from building on existing strengths. Sony does the former with its Walkmans, camcorders and Discmans. Texas Instruments spent years in the 1980s doing the latter with its mania for cost cutting.

A WORD OF CLARIFICATION

There are always some people, at least, at management seminars, or in book reviews, who draw the following conclusion from what has just been set out in the above section: 'You are telling us that there is no point in bothering with the long-term future because it is unknowable. All we have to do is manage the short term as tightly as possible and then be ready to react flexibly to whatever else happens. Basically, there is little we can do but reduce our risk exposure and leave the long term to take care of itself.'

This response means that the person making it is still looking at the world through the lenses of the old stable equilibrium organisation. From that perspective, abandoning visions and long-term plans means abandoning all concern with the long term. But this is most emphatically *not* the message of a far-from-equilibrium model of how to manage strategically.

This new model means looking at things from a different perspective. The message is about handling, here and now, issues having widespread and long-term consequences in a different, more innovative, more creative way – not abandoning such concerns. And that more creative way is a process of real-time complex learning, not the static linear activity of planning. Let me explain what this means.

Most of us immediately think of learning as an individual activity which occurs out of real time. So, we learn when we take time off from real life to attend lectures, read textbooks or analyse some problem. The formulation of visions and the preparation of long term plans well in advance of action is just this kind of learning. We go away for weekends to country retreats in order to develop mission statements and prepare plans. And then we return to the office on a Monday morning and act in real time according to the mission and the plan.

But there is of course a far more important form of learning that we engage in all the time. We also learn every day at the workplace in groups as those groups act to deal with the problems and opportunities of the business. The most important learning we do flows from that trial and error action we take in real time and even more importantly from the way we reflect on that action as we take it and after we have taken it. Remember that civilisation is not a plan, but the pause between a stimulus and the response. When we face the unknowable we cannot learn out of real time because by definition we do not know what we are supposed to be learning; we can only learn 'on the hoof' in real time.

Whether we are able to learn in this way or not will depend upon how people interact with each other in groups. It will depend upon group dynamics, not planning systems and mystic visions.

For example, a top executive team may be driven by the dynamics of fight/flight. Here, they alternate between fierce internal rivalry around strategic issues on the one hand and avoiding those issues to head-off the conflict that attention to them would bring, on the other hand. A top team driven by such a dynamic will not deal effectively with strategic issues no matter how intellectually sound any plans may be.

Or another top team, driven by the dynamic of dependence on one charismatic leader, will never surface new ideas. They will simply follow the leader, perhaps to success but perhaps over the cliff.

The strategic choices a top team makes has far more to do with the nature of the dynamic in their group than it does with any rational consideration. And that dynamic depends upon how people use power, how they exert authority, how they fill their roles.

So, when this book claims that visions and long-term plans are fantasy defences against anxiety, it is not recommending that you shut your eyes to the long term. On the contrary, it is inviting you to open your eyes to the only processes that are realistically available for dealing with the unknowable long term: the processes of real time learning in groups, of reasoning by analogy, of relying on intuition. It is directing your attention away from imaginary obstacles such as a lack of information or the absence of techniques and prescriptions. It is directing your attention instead towards the real obstacles which have to do with how power is used and the impact this has on group dynamics and the effectiveness of your organisation's political system.

Furthermore, when you see the world through new lenses you see that you cannot reduce your risk by simply letting the long term take care of itself. Doing little other than that which seems absolutely safe could run much bigger risks than taking a chance. If the consequences of both are unknowable, how can you know? Instead of laying off the risk you will be more inclined to take risks.

The old mentality encourages you to do nothing until you know what will happen. It encourages you to do more of the same in the mean time.

It makes it sound reasonable to do only enough to earn an acceptable rate of return.

The new mentality makes it clear that there is no point in waiting until you know what will happen – you never can. If you think in this way, you know that you cannot lay off the risk and stay in business. You have to take a chance and keep learning.

The new mentality makes it clear that building quality things that last, taking a pride in what is built, makes sense because we can never know in advance what the rate of return will turn out to be.

The new mentality encourages managers to believe that they can create their future, even if they do not know what it will be.

These managers are not ignoring the long term, they are doing creative, daring things and learning from them all the time.

Another response to the new mental model is to say that all these informal group learning and political processes are rather loose and no good for large complex organisations. These, it is argued, must have tight formal systems. Again this response reveals the power of the old mindset. When you look at the world of organising through the new lenses you do not see 'either/or' choices. What you see instead is 'and/both' choices. Successful organisations, that is, continually innovative organisations, cannot choose between tight formal control systems and structures on the one hand and loose informal behaviours that provoke learning on the other. Whether they be large or small, successful organisations have to have both at the same time. This is because all of them have to handle both knowable, closed change and unknowable, open-ended change at the same time. The result is certainly organisational tension and never-ending contradiction, but this provokes conflict and learning and so is the source of creativity.

QUESTIONING MENTAL MODELS

The most daunting task facing managers today lies at a far deeper and more disturbing level than the obvious one of coping with turbulent change. Most managers, preoccupied with stability and obvious forms of control, are not taking sufficient account of the dynamics of business success. The real challenge, therefore, is to develop a more appropriate frame of reference to understand the unstable dynamic of business and design creative actions. It is the mental models managers deploy, not some bag of tools or techniques, that determines their ability to deal with the unknowable.

It is the aim of this book to encourage managers, consultants and researchers to question today's dominant frame of reference – the stable equilibrium organisation. The proposition to be developed is that, because we fail to think explicitly of a successful business as a dynamic feedback system generating complex, unstable behaviour, we also fail to identify the action criteria for continuing success.

The next chapter develops the reasons for concluding that today's dominant frame of reference for understanding a business is inadequate; the reasons why we need a new mindset. The subsequent chapters explore what this new mindset means to the following key questions managers today ask about their task:

- What kind of organisation do we need if we are to be successful in today's obviously unstable conditions?

- What do we need to do to generate continuing creativity and innovation in our business?

- What is strategic thinking and how do we do it in irregular and contentious circumstances?

- How do we establish strategic direction and intention when the future is unknowable?

- How do we control our business strategically when the future is open-ended and unpredictable?

- How do we secure participation and unleash the creative potential of the people in our business?

In everyday business life managers have to answer questions like these in relation to a world that is quite clearly characterised by stability and instability, predictability and unpredictability, regularity and irregularity, contention and consensus, intention and chance. The world they face is intertwined order and disorder. When we try to explain what is going on and design actions flowing from those explanations, we almost always approach the task from the perspective of order. In doing so we greatly under-emphasise the role of disorder. This book is about turning the perspective on its head; looking at the business world from the angle of disorder and how it is intertwined with order.

No doubt the reader will have heard this old joke. One night a woman is walking down a dark street. She comes to a pool of light under a street lamp and sees a man on his knees obviously looking for something. She asks: 'What are you looking for?' He replies, 'A coin I have lost.' 'Well where did you lose it?' she enquires. 'Over there,' he responds, pointing to a dark area between two street lights. 'Why on earth are you looking here, then?' comes her puzzled question. 'Because it is lighter' is his exasperated reply.

An old joke, but it encapsulates the message of this book. We are trying to explain the messy, opportunistic global competition game using mental models which are all about order stability, cohesion, consistency and equilibrium. We are not paying enough attention to the irregular, disorderly, chance nature of the game. We are doing this because it is easier and more secure than feeling about in the dark of explanations which run in terms of disorder, irregularity, unpredictability and chance. This book is concerned with the insights those darker explanations have to give.

REFERENCES

1. De Geus, P (1988) 'Planning as Learning', Harvard Business Review, March-April.

2. Peters, T J & Waterman, R H (1982) *In Search of Excellence*, Harper & Rowe, New York.

3. Pascale, R T (1990) *Managing on the Edge: How Successful Companies use Conflict to Stay Ahead*, Viking Penguin, London.
   Miller, D (1990) *The Icarus Paradox: How Excellent Organizations Can Bring About Their Own Downfall*, Harper Business, New York.
   Hamel, G & Prahalad, C K (1989) 'Strategic Intent', Harvard Business Review, May-June.

4. Miller, op. cit.

5. Senge, P (1990) *The Fifth Discipline*, Doubleday Currency, New York.

6. Senge, P, op. cit.

7. This book gives no information on where or how system dynamics applies to nature's systems or about the mathematics involved. These matters are covered in a highly accessible manner in:
    Gleick, J (1987) *Chaos: Making a New Science*, Heinemann, New York.
    Stewart, I (1989) Does God Play Dice? The Mathematics of Chaos, Blackwell, Oxford.

8. Little attempt is made in this book to explain how the theories of management can be related to modern scientific theories of complex dynamics. I have attempted that in:
    Stacey, R D (1991) *The Chaos Frontier: Creative Strategic Control for Business*, Butterworth-Heinemann, Oxford.

2

Why Managers Need a Different Mindset

When managers design actions to control and develop their business, most do so within a commonly accepted mental framework. Most believe, without questioning, that businesses achieve success by planning to realise some shared vision of the future. The mindset is that of the stable equilibrium organisation following an organisationally intended direction in a centrally controlled manner. This chapter develops the reasons why practical managers now need to question this exclusive focus on stability, regularity, predictability and cohesion. It leads to the design of inadequate responses to the dynamic competition game managers have to play if their organisation is to survive. First, consider the nature of the competitive game and compare it with the prescriptions that today's mindset leads to.

WHAT MANAGERS FACE: ESCALATION AND SELF-REINFORCING CIRCLES

Eastman Kodak has been selling photographic materials in Japan since the late nineteenth century. But after the Second World War it scaled down its operations in what was then a relatively unimportant market. It handed over the marketing of its products to Japanese distributors for political reasons. These actions contributed to the ability of Fuji to build up a 70 per cent share of the Japanese market, leaving Kodak with less than 10 per cent by the beginning of the 1980s. Once it had established a secure position in its home market, Fuji turned its attention to America and Europe, markets where Kodak enjoyed a lucrative dominance in colour film. Throughout the 1980s Kodak suffered the onslaughts of Fuji, forcing it into panic cost-cutting exercises that were not always successful. The Kodak share price under-performed for years, prompting rumours of eventual break-up.

Note how relatively unimportant actions taken years ago have consequences that accumulate slowly to have impacts on geographically distant markets. Cause and effect are distant from each other in time and place.

Then in 1984 Kodak began to strike back. It invested $500m to build up a Japanese operation, regaining control of distribution, encouraging local equity stakes and investing heavily in advertising and promotion. The result has been a sixfold sales increase giving a 15 per cent market share. Even so, the operation is only now making a profit and it will take years to pay back the original investment.

But more important, this invasion has squeezed Fuji's margins in its home market and put it on the defensive in the American and European markets. Fuji has been forced to divert resources from overseas to defend itself at home. This is illustrated on a trivial but amusing scale by the following incident. Kodak spent $1m on an airship sporting its logo. That airship was floated over Fuji's Tokyo head office prompting fun-poking articles in Japanese newspapers. Fuji then had to spend much more than Kodak to bring its own airship from Europe for a face-saving promotion in Tokyo.[1] Note the interactive feedback nature of this competitive game – relatively small actions in one place can precipitate actions and consequences in another, in a self-reinforcing manner.

This tale encapsulates the most immediately obvious problem facing managers today: how to make and enact strategic choices in a highly interconnected and fiercely competitive world. To survive in even the most powerful international companies, managers have to pre-empt, counter, ward off and initiate creative competitive moves continually to attract and retain customers. Managers have to play a fast-moving interactive game, increasingly on a global scale, where the playing conditions and the rules change rapidly. It is a game in which relatively small moves can escalate to have major unexpected consequences. So an attack in one market, which may not be all that important to your business, can have escalating consequences in all the others. During the late 1960s and early 1970s, Japanese companies detected 'loose bricks' in the black and white, and small screen, television set markets in America and Europe. They soon dominated these relatively unattractive segments and used their positions and cash flows in these continents to mount attacks on many other consumer electronics markets.

The game is one in which the players get caught up in self-reinforcing vicious and virtuous circles. Start to lose out in one market and you soon lose out in others. It is a game of gaining a foothold, using a chink or a crack to build small positions that lead to self-reinforcing virtuous circles. The pace of the game has been quickening and will continue to do so – and that game is the same whether it is played in a global setting or a purely local one. It is an unstable game, full of surprises where the outcome cannot be predicted. Success goes to the nimble, the creative, the innovative players whose moves are designed within an understanding of the dynamics of the game: the sometimes gradually accumulating, the sometimes rapidly escalating, patterns of competitive interaction between the players geographically and over time. Winners design their actions accordingly.

Managers, consultants and researchers are all perfectly aware of this. But now consider the approach that the great majority in North America and the UK adopt to prescribing and designing the moves required to win.

HOW MOST MANAGERS BELIEVE THEY SHOULD RESPOND: ORDERLY VISIONS AND PLANS

I recently facilitated a series of workshops with a group of top managers in a company facing a market that was becoming much more competitive than it had ever been before. The purpose of the workshops was to review how those managers were handling the new challenges. They were approaching the game in much the same, explicit way as most of the other competent managers I have worked with in many companies. They found out what their customers thought of them and what those customers now wanted from them. Through market research, they discovered that their major grouping of customers regarded them as a distant company which was inefficient, unresponsive and not user-friendly. What the customers wanted, according to the research, was a company that was innovative in relation to environmental issues, customer care and efficiency. Customers were looking for an assertive, dynamic, proactive company that would work in partnership with them.

The vision

The consultants who carried out this research recommended that the company should develop a corporate market position, image, vision or umbrella brand. The vision, they said, should be one of the company as 'The Innovators'. The consultants described this vision as a framework, blue print, or future direction for focused, consistent and cohesive management decision making. The framework was also to provide a motivating understandable purpose for employees, as well as a strategy for communicating what the company was to stand for in the future to customers, suppliers, shareholders and the media. This corporate vision and image was intended to be an overall guiding framework within which business units would differentiate themselves, and their products, through improved customer care and efficiency. The vision itself was also to differentiate the company from the competition and add value to the company's products and services. Its purpose was to unify the company both internally and externally.

The above paragraphs use the words of the consultants acting in this case. Note the concern with shared, over-arching intention, central control and adapting to the market environment.

The plans

The company turned to other consultants for advice on how to implement such a vision. Here the recommendations were to set up a systematic planning and development process to deliver a strategy of growth within the overall vision. The consultants stressed that implementation problems were the most important causes of failure to achieve plan objectives. Effective implementation required a clear distinction in roles. The principal distinction was to be that between strategic market planning and marketing management. The role of strategic market planning was to be at the corporate level with the following role tasks:

- identifying the growth path of the company with the emphasis on business plans for new ventures;

- advising on allocation of resources between existing business units;

- differentiating the business as a whole by specifying and controlling the vision, or umbrella brand.

The role of marketing management was to be at the business unit level, with the following role tasks:

- identifying market segments;

- differentiating the products of the existing businesses;

- controlling the marketing mix within the overall corporate image, vision or brand.

The result was to be the preparation of three levels of plans – the corporate plan, the business unit plans and the product plans. These plans were to be implemented so as to achieve the vision indicated by the phrase 'The Innovators'. To sum up, the consultants were clearly recommending that actions should be be centrally controlled according to a shared overall intention to which all in the organisation should be committed. The emphasis was quite clearly on:

- order

- stability

- consistency

- control.

Once again the words used in the above paragraphs are those used by the consultants in this case. Note the concern with analytical techniques, step by step thinking, order and harmony.

DOES AN ORDERLY, CONSISTENT APPROACH SQUARE WITH ESCALATING, SELF-REINFORCING GAMES?

At the particular meeting where the above proposals were discussed, they were treated with limited scepticism by some, but there was certainly no outright rejection. Over the past few years I have seen very similar proposals treated in much same way, over and over again. They represent a widely received, if sometimes uneasily accepted, wisdom on the part of both managers and the consultants they look to for advice.

On the face of it, however, this overview on how to play the competitive game in an orderly consistent manner sits rather uneasily with the earlier description of that game as a fast-moving, messy one of escalation and self-reinforcing circles full of surprises and unpredictable outcomes. On the face of it, today's received wisdom sounds like a rather static approach to playing a very dynamic game. The game is dynamic, interactive and nonlinear, moving in circles with cause and effect distant from each other. The recommended response is based on linear, straight line thinking with close links between intention and outcome.

That the game and the response do not match all that well is confirmed by the way in which managers actually carry out the prescriptions and the consequences this has. Consider first what they actually do.

HOW MOST MANAGERS ACTUALLY RESPOND: CURIOUS BEHAVIOUR

When managers act within the frameworks set out above, they do a number of things that are, on the face of it anyway, rather curious.

Obvious 'visions' and 'objectives'

Managers frequently enunciate visions that are perfectly obvious. In the case outlined above, managers were talking about a vision of being 'Innovative'. But if the market game nowadays is a fast-moving, highly competitive and uncertain one, then surely success demands innovative behaviour on the part of all the players. It is difficult to see how much the 'Innovators' vision differentiates a company from any of its successful rivals.

Other examples of visions have to do with beating the competition, or caring for customers, or delivering quality and high service levels. Again these are concerns every company has to attend to, if it wishes to survive. They are continuing rules of the game, not long-term objectives towards which the company should be moving. If you are not doing them already there may well be no long term for your business.

You do not need to envision anything at all to know that innovation, competitive capability, quality, customer care and good service are all essential. The word 'vision' implies an ability to see something about the shape of a future market; something managers can use to design their actions in advance of that state materialising. In practice, however, most management visions turn out to be ambitions or aspirations, or they may be simply an interpretation of the issue currently commanding the most management attention. Even more frequently, a vision is an interpretation of the cause of some successful outcome made with the benefit of hindsight.

Objectives are more precise than visions. But when you look at examples of long-term objectives, you usually find that they are statements about target growth rates in sales or profit, or target rates of return on capital. Again these are simply rules of the game, if managers wish their organisation to survive as a separate entity. You do not have to know anything about the future to set these targets.

Managers talk about the need for vision and objectives in general as if they are some future state to be achieved, but in specific terms they articulate instead the current rules of the competitive game, their current ambitions and the current issues attracting their attention.

Changing objectives

As managers try to set more specific long-term goals or objectives, they qualify them with statements such as, 'objectives must not be cast in tablets of stone', or 'they must not be set in aspic'. In other words, long-term strategic objectives are to be loose and they will be changed long before we reach the time any specific objective was first intended to apply to. If this is so, it follows that in reality managers are discovering their objectives as they move through time. They are not setting them well in advance as stable guides to actions with long-term consequences – yet they talk about the need for actions to be driven by stable, prior strategic intention. Saying that we must have long-term objectives and then continually changing them is a curiously illogical form of behaviour.

Plans not implemented

Next, managers set out long-term plans for the next five years but in effect these plans are frequently out of date within six months. Five years later, the company finds it has done something completely different from what it set out to do. This observation leads to the response that, of course, long-term plans will have to be continually changed. It must then be legitimate to ask whether they are five year plans at all. A plan is a sequence of intended actions established before action is undertaken. If managers keep changing that intended sequence then in fact they are discovering what to do as they go along. It seems strange and illogical behaviour, setting out a sequence of actions for a particular time period in the full knowledge that this is not the sequence to be enacted. We say that we need to establish shared organisation-wide intention and set out sequences of intended actions, but in fact we discover both intentions and actions as we go along.

Lack of monitoring

When it comes to monitoring, the whole long-term planning process becomes even more curious. In a recent study of the top 250 companies in the UK, only 11 per cent of the sample replying to a questionnaire said that they set long-term milestones and then monitored performance against them. In-depth interviews with a number of companies in the sample revealed that even fewer monitored their strategic plans in a formal way, and those that did so classed events such as building a new factory, rather than some results based milestone.[2] Now, if no one is monitoring their long-term plans effectively, they cannot be using them as a form of long-term control. On the one hand managers maintain that it is necessary to prepare long-term plans to enable top management to control the long-term direction of the business. On the other hand, we find that the great majority still do not use them as the control system they are proposed to be.

In practice plans are vague and not comprehensive

In my own personal experience as a management consultant, I have found a number of characteristic features in companies with long-term plans. Despite the existence of a plan, large numbers of managers, even at the top, are unable to give an account of the future strategy of the company. When they do so it often conflicts with those given by their colleagues. And those accounts are rarely specific enough to constitute clear intentions and lists of specific actions that are to be taken in the future.

When one looks at the documents embodying those plans, they are usually a set of long-term financial projections that nobody believes, accompanied by lists of strengths and weaknesses, opportunities and threats, from which one can draw little in the way of conclusions.

When specific strategic issues arise and are dealt with, managers very rarely refer back to the long-term plan they have just prepared. Even if they do the issue is usually not to be found in the plan. Despite what is supposed to be an overall control framework, they continue to handle specific strategic issues on a one-by-one basis.

DCF appraisals manipulated

Similar observations can be made about the manner in which other management techniques are used in practice. Only a minority of managers appraise investments using the widely prescribed discounted cash flow techniques. However, even those that do, do so in a curious way. When I listen to discussions on whether to proceed with the investment, I hear managers say: 'Of course the one thing we do know, is that none of these figures will come true'; or 'Don't worry too much about the net present value, we will find a few more synergies to bump it up. The point is, do you think that this is a worthwhile investment?'. One must then ask why managers bother with these calculations in the first place when they know that something else will materialise and when they seem to have so few qualms about manipulating the figures to correspond with their judgment.

Cohesion not maintained

There is widespread agreement amongst managers that success requires them to work together in cohesive teams. There is also general agreement that politics and conflict should be avoided and that decisions should be made using rational processes. Managers do not like talking about power and the impact this has on behaviour and decision making. Despite this agreement, managers continue to conflict and make decisions on an internal political basis. Despite their explicit reluctance to discuss the behavioural dynamics of their interaction with each other, those dynamics exert a major impact on the decisions taken.

Top management not in control

Finally, the whole point of the vision and planning frameworks, based on the belief in order, harmony and cohesive teams, is that those at the top will then be in control of the company's destiny. But when you talk informally to highly competent managers you hear them referring to 'luck' and 'chance'. One manager I worked with had just installed a major reorganisation of his company and he said, 'We will have to wait and see if it works'. A divisional managing director I was speaking to expressed this view – 'The chief executive can't really control what the guys do in the market place and neither can I'. Another chief executive expressed this concern – 'What makes me nervous is that my colleagues keep agreeing with me. If they don't argue back, I could end up doing something really wrong'. Despite their visions and their plans, competent managers recognise that they are not in control of long-term outcomes, that chance is important, and that continuing consensus is undesirable.

So, managers do not actually implement the plan and vision prescriptions as they are intended to be implemented. Nevertheless, many try to do so – and because they design their actions within this mindset, they do so in curious ways that have a number of unfortunate consequences.

WHAT THE CONSEQUENCES ARE: IMITATION AND EXCESS

When managers think of strategy as plan, they are by definition focusing their attention on securing a widely shared commitment to achieve a foreseeable future state. They are focusing their attention on a pattern in actions that is cohesive, consistent and integrating. They are trying to produce regularity and to sustain stable equilibrium, both internally and externally. This is what planning means. This mentality has major consequences for the actions managers will then design.

In practice, actions and their consequences are only regular and foreseeable when they represent repetitions of the past; repetitions of what managers have done and are already doing well. The planning mentality therefore leads managers to design actions that reinforce the direction already established for the business. That mentality leads managers to build on their strengths, stick to their core businesses and make only small, logically incremental changes. When managers focus on the predictable, their actions are predictable too.

A number of studies spell out the harmful consequences of this focus. In their Harvard Business Review Article,[3] Hamel and Prahalad report on their study of a number of global and multinational companies. They conclude that the planning concepts of strategic fit with the environment, hierarchies of goals and strategies and regular patterns of differentiation versus low cost, have led to competitive decline. Companies pursuing this approach tend to imitate their rivals and soon fall prey to more imaginative ones. Based on studies of a great many companies, both Miller[4] and Pascale[5] conclude that successful companies fail with great frequency because they take to excess that which made them successful in the first place. Because they continue to focus on their strengths, they miss new directions and eventually fail. The planning mentality leads to imitation and concentration of effort on the knowable.

What managers are doing, therefore, is excluding the possibility of continuing creativity and innovation. Innovation is, by definition, a break with the past and the outcome is unpredictable. Creativity requires irregularity and instability to shatter old perceptions and patterns of behaviour, so making way for the new.

This argument is strengthened when we consider the circumstances in which managers are most able to secure continuing shared commitment. People will more readily share commitment to an aim, policy or course of action, and continue to do so, when they can foresee the consequences for themselves, their organisation and the part of it that most concerns them. People will find it very difficult to share commitment when they face ambiguous, open-ended issues. By insisting on prior shared intention and regular patterns of action, the planning mentality actually predisposes people to avoid open-ended issues with unknowable future consequences. Planning contains a built-in bias to continue down already established paths of action.

The planning concept is so attractive and we cling to it tenaciously, because we want to avoid unpleasant surprises. The planning concept encourages managers to believe that they can avoid surprises. As soon as they cannot foresee the outcome of a proposed action, the tendency is to talk about laying off the risk: that means, getting someone else to bear it. They talk about letting others develop highly risky new products first and then they will enter the market when the risk level is lower. The planning mentality develops a bias against taking risks. Discounted cash flow investment appraisal methods reinforce this bias because the calculations cannot include unforeseeable benefits from an innovation. These attitudes towards risk discourage innovation because that is an essentially risky activity.

To approach conditions of turbulent change and unknowable futures with a mental model based on the plan concept, is a recipe for repetition and the avoidance of creativity and innovation. It provides dangerous false comfort because when managers prepare plans, they believe that they are dealing with the strategic. It is then easy to ignore the need to reflect upon the political processes and learning activities that actually determine their strategic responses.

The harmful consequences of visions

The insistence that managers should develop a vision or dream of what their organisation as a whole is to be at some point in the future also has a number of harmful consequences.

First, if you advise managers to envisage a picture of a future state, they do not know what to do and if they believe they must, it inhibits action. The advice to form a vision is neither concrete enough to be useful, nor is it possible when the future is unknowable.

For example, take a group of divisional managers I worked with recently. The division consisted of a number of information technology companies that had been acquired a short time before. Some of these companies distributed directly to end users and others sold products to own equipment manufacturers, including their sister subsidiaries. The direct distribution companies therefore competed with customers of those who distributed products indirectly. Not surprisingly, this use of two routes to market led to continual conflict between the subsidiaries. Those distributing through the indirect route complained that those distributing directly were competing unfairly because of the transfer pricing rules imposed by the division. This was antagonising the customers of those distributing indirectly and they were therefore losing business. The problem confronting the divisional management was therefore either one of devising an organisational structure and transfer pricing policies to allow both companies to operate effectively, or to abandon one of the routes to market.

To deal with the problem divisional management were advised to formulate a vision or dream of what they wanted to be in the future. The mission statement they all agreed upon was to become one of the major players in the market, using both routes to market if that turned out to be the right thing to do. Given the uncertain market conditions they faced, none of the divisional managers felt that they were able to formulate anything more specific than this. What they really came up with was a 'wait and see how it turns out' posture. There was nothing in this to indicate which structural form or what transfer pricing policy was appropriate. Instructing these managers to have a vision had no practical use and indeed distracted attention from the real issue. The real issue was about conflicting ambitions on the part of the members of the team and judgements about the reactions of the own equipment customers and competitors to different arrangements. Focusing on the 'here and now' strategic issue agenda was possible and practical, while formulating visions was not.

In addition, this advice to form a vision had a debilitating effect on some of the managers involved. The managing director of the division decided to use a workshop approach with middle managers to surface their views on what form the reorganisation should take. The first meeting of this workshop did not reach agreement – one reason for this was the different assumptions people were making about the future direction of the business. In particular, one group was assuming that the major future impetus would be through sales of their products direct to the end users, while another was assuming that the main thrust would be through indirect sales to own equipment manufacturers. They looked to top management to make a decision about future direction. But the top management team stated that they did not know where the future direction lay – it was all too uncertain.

At the next workshop, some of the middle managers found this completely unacceptable; they could not see how any further work on reorganisation could continue without first defining future direction. In fact, the group as a whole was able to put forward sensible proposals about reorganisation to deal with the here and now. But some members were demotivated; their contribution declined because of their belief in the need for future direction.

The second defect of the vision prescription has already been referred to. If you insist that managers should all share a common view of their future without question, you invite them to persist with what they already know how to do. Or, you encourage them to pursue what could be a disastrous new idea in a lemming-like dash to destruction, and while they are doing this, they will inevitably overlook other changes.

Third, the advice on visions places a tremendous and unrealistic burden on the 'leader'. It perpetuates the myth that organisations have to rely on one or two unusually gifted individuals to decide what to do, while the rest enthusiastically follow. This advice perpetuates cultures of dependence and conformity that actually obstruct the questioning and complex learning which encourages innovative action.

Fourth, the vision advice distracts attention from what people are really doing when they successfully handle unknowable futures – learning and political interaction. If you talk to managers about strategy as pattern in action determined by visionary or planning activity, there is immediate recognition of what you are talking about. If you talk about strategy as pattern in action emerging from learning and political activity, you are frequently greeted with blank stares. And yet it is the latter, I believe, that managers actually do when they manage strategically.

WHY ARE MANAGERS NOT IMPLEMENTING THE PRESCRIPTIONS AS INTENDED?

So far then, we have reached three conclusions:

1. The widely prescribed vision and plan frameworks are not all that consistent with the dynamic interactive competition game.

2. Managers act in ways indicating that although they espouse these frameworks, they are not using them as intended.

3. Because they are nevertheless frequently designing their actions from this perspective, they produce harmful consequences.

Why are visions and plans not delivering the future pictures, over shared intention, control, stability and consensus their proponents claim they do? Why are harmful consequences produced? Why do most managers keep proclaiming the importance of thinking about the future, intentionally setting future direction and planning for the long term, and then either failing to prepare plans, or to implement the plans they prepare, or to monitor the outcomes? We can no longer say that this is because managers themselves do not prepare the plans. Nowadays they, rather than staff planners, do. The failure of long-term planning cannot be due to a lack of techniques and analytical frameworks with which to formulate plans – the literature on strategic planning and positioning is now huge. The failure cannot still be due to a lack of expertise in this area – a significant consultancy industry exists to provide it, more and more top managers have been to business schools and understand perfectly well what is required of a long-term planning system. We have to look for other reasons. Some find those reasons in market pressures, company policies or behavioural obstacles.

The problem is short-termism

Perhaps the most persistent criticism of management, at least in the USA and the UK, is that managers are far too concerned with short-term profitability. Indeed, many managers themselves put forward this view and managers and critics alike ascribe such short-termism to the manner in which the financial markets operate. The well known argument is this. Companies in America and the UK depend primarily upon equity capital for their financing. The major providers of this finance are institutional fund managers whose performance is measured against very short-term quarterly share price criteria: consequently they demand high short-term profit levels. As a result, managers in industry and commerce have no option but to take a short-term view if they are to avoid undervalued shares and attendant takeover risks. Consequently managers will avoid taking decisions that have long pay-back periods or high levels of risk. The financial market pressures compel managers to avoid innovative long-term behaviour. This is why, it is claimed, we find that most companies have short-term planning or budgetary systems but fail to use long-term planning effectively. This is why most managers, it is believed, do not appraise capital projects using rational discounted cash flow techniques.[6]

Now, while this argument is widely canvassed by the press, frequently put forward by academics and supported by many managers (perhaps because it puts most of the blame on the financial institutions), there does not seem to be very strong evidence to support it. First, there is not much evidence that fund managers behave in a manner conditioned entirely by the next three months – they have careers to think about that extend past the next three months. If they build portfolios of shares in companies which simply make a fast buck, they may achieve good performance for a short while, but the whole portfolio could well collapse after that. Secondly, studies have shown that share prices rise when companies announce major investment or research and development programmes.[7] It may well be something of a myth that stock markets force managers to behave in short-term ways.

The studies debunking this myth tend to put the blame for short-termism on the managers of industrial and commercial companies. The argument is that short-termism is the consequence of reward structures tied to short-term profit performance, the lack of effective control based on long-term planning and the widespread use of pay-back investment appraisal techniques having a short-term bias. The implication is that if managers changed reward structures, adopted longer term planning forms of control and appraised investments using discounted cash flow techniques, all would be well. But does this make sense? While managers will undoubtedly be much concerned about this year's profit, especially when their bonuses are tied to it, they will also be concerned about the rest of their careers. It is not much good getting a high bonus this year and perhaps next, if the company goes under thereafter. And it *will* go under if managers are concerned only with short-term profits. It seems absurd to believe that they are not aware of this.

The problem is politics

Yet another criticism lays the blame for ineffective long-term planning at the door of internal politics. The argument here is that managers take decisions which will progress their own careers even if those decisions are not in the company's best interests. By trying to build departmental and business unit empires, managers obstruct the formulation and implementation of sensible long-term plans and the achievement of visions. But is it realistic or sensible to see political activity in a business organisation as the result purely of self-seeking?

The claim, then, is that managers do not use long-term plans effectively because the financial markets discourage it, or because managers themselves are incredibly short-sighted, or because they play selfish politics. These claims simply do not seem to hold up. Because managers are failing to use widely prescribed frameworks does not necessarily prove that these managers do not handle issues with long-term consequences. It does not mean that they are blithely unconcerned with survival. If managers are not actually using these frameworks as they are intended to be used, it may well be because the frameworks themselves are inappropriate.

Despite the problems, some say the frameworks have their benefits

Some will say that even though the vision and planning frameworks do not deliver the stability and control they are supposed to, the process of arriving at them is vital. They are useful provokers of strategic thinking. If this is so, then we would expect to find some evidence that long-term planning improves performance.

But there is little evidence that long-term planning improves performance

When we compare those companies who do utilise a strategic planning approach with those who do not, there is no reliable evidence that the former perform better. Greenley[8] recently surveyed nine studies which had looked for a connection between strategic planning and performance in manufacturing companies.

Eight of these studies were carried out in the US and one in the UK. Sample sizes varied from 10 to 386 companies. Five studies concluded that there is a connection between strategic planning and performance and four failed to find any positive evidence. After excluding studies with more obvious methodological deficiencies, there was one study which found a connection between planning and performance and another which found none. Both studies applied to the US – and both studies can be criticised. Other factors, besides planning, affect performance and these cloud the connection, or lack of it, between planning and performance. It is not clear whether planning leads to good performance, or whether good performance generates the funds with which to plan. The statistical tests used to identify a connection between planning and performance contain subjective judgements on how formal or otherwise the planning system is. Therefore we can draw no reliable conclusion from the evidence as to whether strategic planning improves performance or not, even after forty years of prescribing it.

However, there are many studies reporting close links between managers with visions and successful organisations. It will be argued in Chapter 6 that much of this evidence is concerned with visions that have a meaning other than some picture of a future state. It will also be argued that the link researchers keep finding between success and vision as a picture of a future state, is simply a reflection of the stable equilibrium mindset those researchers approach their task with.

There is, then, little clear evidence that planning and envisioning are linked to superior performance or that they provoke creative strategic thinking. The reasons given for the failure of managers to use these frameworks properly do not stand up. So, what is the problem? The problem, I believe, lies in the mental models we use to interpret business behaviour.

THE PROBLEM IS THE MINDSET: DIRECT CAUSE AND EFFECT LINKS

Management experts operate in the same manner as all other experts and when they interpret business situations they employ mental models which are very rarely examined; they are simply taken to be true. So, both the managers and the consultants at the company described on pages 35–37 were employing a particular model to design actions to differentiate the company and its products from the competition. They were assuming without question that success is to be secured by fixing on some vision or image, preparing plans to achieve it, motivating people to believe in and cohere around it. The critics of management today are employing the same mental model to design their criticisms. They claim that managers are in some sense performing inadequately because they are not setting clear long-term objectives, they are not preparing long-term plans, and even when they do they are not monitoring those plans or implementing them.

The argument to be developed in the rest of this book is that managers are not using visions and long-term plans as intended; that their curious behaviour occurs because the frameworks of visions and plans are inappropriate to the open-ended situations in which strategic issues arise. In those situations, successful managers in fact proceed in other ways. And we fail to pay much explicit attention to these other ways because most of us are using inadequate mental models to interpret the dynamics of business behaviour.

Underlying today's mental models there is the unquestioned assumption that the effects we observe can be directly linked to causes in a straightforward, linear fashion. We are assuming that our actions and their outcomes can, in principle at least, be unequivocally linked to each other. It is this basic assumption that leads us to a number of beliefs that govern what we look for when we research, what we prescribe and what management actions we design. Most of us believe that:

- the vehicle for success is the stable equilibrium organisation;
- techniques and systems can be installed in advance to secure innovative success;
- strategic thinking is an analytical process;
- strategy is a regular pattern in action flowing from organisational intention;
- control is negative feedback keeping the organisation on a predetermined, regular path;
- more innovative activity can be secured when people are encouraged to participate through flexible structures, loose job definitions and distributed power.

Each of these ideas is discussed separately in the six chapters that follow. The purpose will be to show how a mindset conditioned by understanding modern dynamic system complexity leads us to the opposite perspective in each case. It leads us to see that the only purpose long-term plans serve is that of a rational defence against the anxiety provoked by great uncertainty. It also leads us to see that visions and shared values are mystic defences against that same uncertainty. The new perspective leads us to abandon these defences and instead focus our attention on the learning and political interaction which constitutes real strategic management; the mode managers use to undertake the innovative journey of exploration into the unknowable future.

REFERENCES

1. The Economist, November 1990.

2. Goold, M with Quinn, J J (1990) *Strategic Control: Milestones for Long Term Performance*, Hutchinson, London.

3. Hamel, G & Prahalad, C K (1989) Strategic Intent, Harvard Business Review, May-June.

4. Miller, D (1990) *The Icarus Paradox: How Excellent Companies Bring About Their Own Downfall*, Harper Collins, London.

5. Pascale, R T (1990) *Managing on the Edge: How Successful Companies Use Conflict to Stay Ahead*, Viking Penguin, London.

6. London Business School survey reported in the Financial Times on 7 November 1990, showed that two thirds of companies used pay-back methods.

7. Marsh, P (1990) Short Termism on Trial, Institutional Fund Managers Association, London.

8. Greenley, G E (1986) Does Strategic Planning Improve Company Performance?, *Long Range Planning*, 19, No. 2.

3

Systems, Success and Instability

A common theme runs through the way in which the media treat just about any business these days. During periods of rapidly improving performance, the media build a company and its top managers into business folk heroes. As soon as performance falters, the media knock them down again. During the mid-1980s, in the UK, newspapers were full of praise for the business folk heroes of the Thatcher era. To name but a few, there were Ralph Halpern who transformed sleepy Hepworths into a modern chain of men's fashion stores; George Davies who developed an innovative new retail concept in the Next chain of fashion stores; and Alan Sugar who built up the Amstrad consumer electronics empire. Today Hepworths and Next together with their principal architects are seen as 'has beens'. Alan Sugar and Amstrad also come in for periodic criticism.

We see the same phenomenon in the USA. Ford Motor Company is praised for its business skill during some periods and written off in others. General Electric is held up as a model for all to follow in some periods and then knocked down as an overweight conglomerate during others. The criteria for praise and condemnation are clear. Companies and their managers are only excellent when they display consistently stable improvements in their performance.

EXCELLENCE AS CONSISTENTLY STABLE PERFORMANCE

It is not only sensation-seeking newspapers and television programmes that interpret excellence as consistency in performance. This perspective provides the underlying assumption made by those who make serious attempts to try to identify what it is that makes a company excellent. One of the best known examples of this search is provided by the Peters and Waterman study which they described in their book 'In Search of Excellence'.[1] They identified a number of companies that were widely regarded as 'state of the art' in management terms. These were companies, such as Boeing, Dupont, Kodak, Atari and Avon, that had shown consistent improvement in profitability and continuing innovative product and technology development. The study identified common features in the management practice of those companies and then prescribed the installation of those features in other companies seeking excellence.

But within five years, two thirds of that sample could no longer be described as excellent – consistent profit and product improvement had faltered. At the time of the study IBM was regarded as an excellent company. Then it was widely judged to be 'dead'. By the late 1980s it was once again being acclaimed as an example to the rest of the business world.

Does it make sense continually to change our judgement in this way? To answer the question we need to examine why we equate stability and excellence.

Instability due to incompetence

There is a widespread assumption on the part of those with immediate comments to hand, and also on the part of more serious analysts, that irregularities in company performance are due to the incompetence of the top management team. It is a view shared by equity holders and top managers themselves – any serious faltering in performance is usually followed by a rapid change in chief executive and key members of the board. If we adopt this assumption that irregular business performance is primarily a consequence of incompetence, then we look for the organisational structures, control systems, cultures, management styles, managerial skills and leadership characteristics that constitute competence. We draw the conclusion that if we can identify the elements of competence and install them, then we will be able largely to banish unstable business performance.

In the UK this identification of management competencies is being put on a formal footing by the Management Charter Initiative, supported by some of the major companies in the country. This Initiative has identified what are regarded as the key competencies required at different levels in the management hierarchy. Having done this, management education programmes are being designed to develop managers with the necessary competencies. Since unstable performance is thought to be due to management incompetence, we seek to remove it and so secure stability.

Instability due to ignorance

We know of course, that even if we do succeed in comprehensively identifying and installing the elements of competence, we will still not banish performance instability altogether. Future changes in the markets, and other aspects of the environment within which companies have to operate, cannot be forecast with complete accuracy. Every business, therefore, will be hit from time to time by unforeseen, random shocks from its environment. Oil prices may rise and fall in unexpected ways, as might interest and exchange rates. Customer requirements and technologies may also develop in unforeseen ways. As a result, unstable business performance will be generated by what amounts to ignorance. Because managers are ignorant of the random shocks coming from the environment, their businesses will exhibit irregularities in performance no matter how competent they are. But ignorance can be conquered, to some extent at least, by gathering and processing more information, by applying more sophisticated forecasting techniques and conducting more research. Competent managers will then seek to overcome ignorance as far as they are able to. They will turn as many apparently random shocks as possible into predictable events and design actions to deal with them in advance of the changes occurring. Competent managers, we believe, think about the future and follow logical steps to deal with it. Competent managers seek to banish ignorance and thus secure stability.

Since instability is the consequence of incompetence and ignorance it must be, quite clearly, the enemy of success. So runs today's received wisdom. But is the unstable business performance we observe really due only to some combination of ignorance and incompetence?

New discoveries about dynamic systems

The discovery of the chaotic and self-organising behaviour of dynamic systems, already referred to in Chapter 1, must lead us to challenge the view that irregular performance is due solely to incompetence and ignorance. Where the behaviour of a system is driven by certain kinds of feedback mechanism, that system's performance or behaviour may be unstable purely because of the structure of the feedback mechanism itself. Instability of a particular kind is a fundamental property of the structure of commonly found feedback mechanisms. Far from being the enemy of success, this particular structural instability is vital to the ability of the system to be continually creative. Consequently, it is necessary to sustain the system in the conditions in which such instability occurs, instead of trying to remove it. For without instability, the system will be incapable of developing new, innovative forms of behaviour. It will be trapped into endlessly repeating its past and existing behaviour.

This discovery means that if a business system is driven by feedback mechanisms of the particular kind these scientists are talking about, then its performance could be unstable for reasons that have to do with the very structure of the business system itself. If this conclusion applied to a business, it would mean that even if we totally banished both incompetence and ignorance (random shocks from the environment), the performance of the business would still display instability. Indeed, a business would have to exhibit instability if it was to be innovative. Systems, success and instability would be intimately interconnected.

If this is true then the judgement that IBM is excellent one year and dead the next is both completely trivial and also dangerously misleading. We would expect and require an excellent company such as IBM to have ups and downs in performance, and display signs of instability, simply because of its feedback nature and the need to innovate. No amount of information gathering, analysis, research and forward planning would be capable of altering this necessary instability. Nor would the acquisition of all the competencies in the world on the part of managers. If these discoveries have anything to do with business we would have to re-examine many of the most fundamental views we currently hold about the requirements for business success.

It is important, from a practical viewpoint, to consider whether or not a business is a feedback system, and whether it is the kind of feedback system to which the new understanding of complex dynamics applies. If a business is such a feedback system it becomes a matter of practical importance to identify the conditions in which it will display inherent structural instability of the kind required for continuing creativity. These considerations are of practical importance because the actions managers design depend on what they believe about the nature of success. If they believe that instability is an inherent and necessary feature of a successful business they will seek to provoke certain kinds of instability. If they believe that instability is due simply to incompetence and ignorance, and is hence the enemy of success, they will seek to banish all forms of instability. And if they make the wrong judgement in this regard, their organisation will not survive.

So, is a business a feedback system of that kind to which the new scientific discoveries apply?

THE IMPORTANCE OF FEEDBACK SYSTEMS IN BUSINESS

It is not difficult to see that every business is, in a fundamental sense, a set of feedback mechanisms. Every business uses the cash flow generated by its sales of yesterday to purchase the inputs it will require for its value adding activities today. Those activities enable the sales which generate the cash flow required for value adding activities tomorrow. Cash moves in a loop over time with inflows being fed back into outflows, in turn generating new inflows.

The same point applies to output levels. Part of yesterday's output is siphoned off to meet orders and the rest feeds into inventories (or backlogs) which play an important part in deciding on output levels today. When the inventories rise we cut output levels and when the backlogs rise we raise output levels. And today's consequent output levels feed back into inventories (or backlogs) and hence tomorrow's output level decisions. Output moves in a loop over time that connects the level in one period to that in another.

Every performance indicator of a business can be thought of as a feedback loop, because every indicator is interconnected with all the others and all are subject to time lags. Conducting a business is simply moving around a large number of interconnected sales; output, input, cash flow and profit feedback loops.

Business performance over time is driven by feedback mechanisms. But are these feedback mechanisms of that type to which the new discoveries of complex dynamics apply?

The profit feedback loop

The answer is yes. And to see this, consider what we might describe as the summary feedback loop of them all – profit. The profit that a company earns in a previous time period plays an important part in the decisions about product offerings made in this time period. Typically, managers decide to plough back the profit of the previous time period into expenditures now, and these expenditures result in product offerings in this time period. So, previous profit is ploughed back into working capital, into capital expenditure, into research and development, into advertising and promotion, and so on. The profit ploughed back may be bolstered by borrowing and the capacity to do this will be related in some way to profitability. Profit in the previous period therefore leads, through a decision making process, to product offerings in this period. And these product offerings lead to the profit of the next period, the link being provided by the response of customers, competitors and suppliers to the product offering and its input requirements. Relationships between any business and the organisations and people that constitute its environment will therefore determine the profit which product offerings will yield. That profit will be fed back into the loop to determine the product offerings to be made in the next period. This loop is depicted in Figure 3.1 opposite.

Profit then, is driven by a mechanism in which profit in one period is fed into profit in the next and the link between them is provided by the decision making behaviour of people within the company, and by the relationships those people have with people in other organisations as well as with individuals. People in other organisations and individuals both constitute a company's environment. The development of a company over time depends upon the interactive relationships between them.

Nonlinear feedback

The important point about this profit feedback loop is this. The links are such that profit in one period is not related to that in another in a straight line or proportional way. The feedback mechanism is a non-proportional or nonlinear one. If the decision making process was such that managers always ploughed back a constant proportion of profit, into, say, working

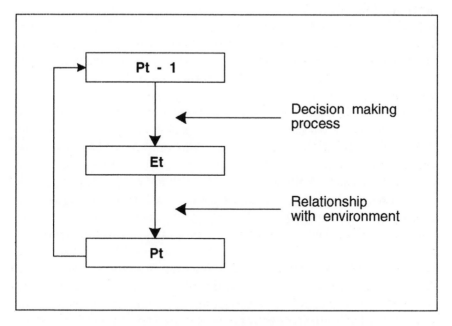

Figure 3.1 The profit feedback loop

capital, and the consequent output of product always brought in a constant proportion of profit, then profit in one period would always bear a straight line, proportional relationship to profit in the next. Suppose managers always plough back 1.2 times last period's profit into working capital. Suppose also that this working capital always results in a profit of 1.5 times that working capital. Then if the starting level of profit is 100, working capital in the next period will be 120 and it will yield profit of 180. The period after that will also see a further 80 per cent increase in profit, and so on.

But of course such linear relationships do not occur in practice. First, decision making rules are such that each time around the loop, managers will allocate less and less extra profit to any one expenditure category. This is because of the law of diminishing returns. The more extra money that is put into research and development, for example, the smaller the additional benefits it brings. The same applies to advertising, capital expenditure, working capital and most other expenditure categories. Also, managers will be prevented from following simple proportional decision rules by financing constraints, limited capacity, skill and materials shortages. Furthermore, when we turn to relationships with the environment, the more product we offer the less additional profit it brings in because we have to lower prices to encourage extra demand. The relationship between profit in one period and profit in another must, therefore, be non-proportional, that is, nonlinear.

The profit feedback loop is nonlinear because its operation is constrained by fundamental economic laws of demand and diminishing returns, by diseconomies of scale and by constraints on finance, capacity, skills and many more. And it is not just performance that is driven by nonlinear feedback. Control and decision making processes are feedback loops in which the outcomes of a decision are fed back into subsequent decisions. Relationships between people in a business and people in their environments are feedback loops too. So, when managers make a product offering, customers and competitors respond and this response feeds back into modifications to the product offering. In all these cases, people typically under- and over-react, making the feedback loops nonlinear.

The discoveries scientists have made about the structural instability of feedback loops, about their complex dynamics, apply to nonlinear ones. These discoveries must therefore, potentially at least, have something to say about the operation of business systems. But before discussing these discoveries it will be helpful to consider how we usually think about the operation of feedback loops.

NEGATIVE AND POSITIVE FEEDBACK – STABILITY AND EXPLOSIVE INSTABILITY

We normally think in terms of only two forms of feedback – negative and positive. Or, to put it another way, we distinguish between feedback that dampens the behaviour of a system and feedback that amplifies it. We see these as two distinct forms of behaviour; an 'either/or' choice for a system.

Negative feedback

Negative or damping feedback is the mechanism that is widely used for automatic control or regulation. Frequently quoted examples of negative feedback are the central heating control system in a house and the governor on a steam engine. In the case of heating control, a desired temperature is set in the control mechanism which also contains a device to sense the room temperature. When the room temperature falls below the desired level, then the control sensor detects this and the control system turns the heat on. When the temperature rises above the desired level the opposite happens. By responding to the deviation from the desired level in an opposite or negative way, the control system dampens any movement away from the desired level. The controls keep the room temperature close to a stable level over time.

The same principle applies to the steam engine governor. As the boiler is stoked, steam pressure rises and the engine speeds up. The governor responds to this by opening a valve to release the steam and so pull the engine speed back to a desired level. As soon as the speed falls below the desired level the valve closes, steam pressure rises and the engine speed increases to the desired level. Here too the operation of the control system is such that fluctuations around the desired level are tempered. In this way, predictably stable equilibrium behaviour is preserved.

The decision making process, that is the control system, of a business is quite clearly a feedback one. And we almost always think about it in terms of negative, damping feedback. So, managers fix targets for profits and then prepare their annual plans or budgets, setting out the time path for product volumes, prices and costs that will yield those profit targets. The plans also determine the actions to be taken to secure volumes, prices and cost levels. As the business moves through time, outcomes are measured and compared with the plan projections to yield variances or deviations. Frequent monitoring of those variances prompts corrective action to bring performance indicators back onto their planned paths. Time lags and unforeseen environmental changes mean that the adjustments are never perfect. But when the control system is operating effectively, as it would in an excellent company, the actual out-turn should fluctuate, in a tightly constrained manner, around the planned levels. The scheduling, budgetary and planning control system of a business utilises negative feedback to operate in a damping manner in exactly the same way as central heating controls or steam engine governors. The outcome is the same – the business is kept on its stable, predetermined equilibrium path.

Positive feedback

Positive or amplifying feedback would of course operate in the opposite manner. The system would then develop along a self-reinforcing path taking temperature or engine speed further away from the desired level. A tiny increase in temperature above the desired level would turn on the heat, so increasing the deviation from the desired level. That deviation would result in continued application of heat so that the room temperature rose even further. Eventually, the inhabitants would die of heat exhaustion. In the case of the steam engine, a small increase in engine speed would partially close the valve, raising steam pressure and thus engine speed. The valve would consequently be closed even further, so further increasing the steam pressure and engine speed until the engine blew up.

So, amplifying feedback generates a vicious circle which escalates small changes. We would describe the behaviour of the system as 'runaway' or 'explosive'. The operation of the control system is such that fluctuations are amplified leading to predictable equilibrium behaviour of a highly unstable kind.

Businesses also display amplifying feedback. For example, a service department faced with increasing response times to telephone calls may divert resources from answering letters to answering calls. But then the letter backlogs rise and irate customers phone in to chase up a reply. The telephone response times consequently rise even further. More resources are diverted to deal with the problem and so the amplification continues.

No sane engineer designs engine or heating control systems to act in an amplifying manner and set off on predictably unstable paths to explosion. And no sane manager designs business control systems that could lead to increasingly divergent behaviour such that the organisation simply disintegrates. Therefore we almost always think of control systems, including business controls, in terms of negative or damping feedback to produce regular patterns of behaviour.

The key discovery about the operation of nonlinear feedback loops is that stable equilibrium and explosively unstable equilibrium are not the only forms of behaviour open to such systems. The choice is not between either negative damping feedback, or positive amplifying feedback. Nonlinear systems have a third choice; and this choice is a state far-from-equilibrium; a state of bounded instability in which behaviour has a pattern, but it is irregular.

BOUNDED INSTABILITY – FAR-FROM-EQUILIBRIUM

When a nonlinear feedback system is driven away from stable equilibrium towards the equilibrium of explosive instability, it passes through a phase of bounded instability in which it displays highly complex behaviour. There is what we might think of as a border area between stable equilibrium and unstable equilibrium, and behaviour in this border area has two important characteristics:

1. It is inherently unpredictable.

2. It displays what has been called a 'hidden' pattern.

Chaos is the name that scientists have given to this border area and the behaviour associated with it. It is also known as strange or fractal. Chaos, in its scientific sense, is not utter confusion. It is not explosive instability. It is constrained instability; a combination of order and disorder in which patterns of behaviour continually unfold in unpredictable but yet similar, familiar, yet irregular forms.

Example: the weather system

To fix ideas, consider one example of chaos from the natural world – the weather system. The weather system is driven by nonlinear feedback mechanisms. Tiny changes in air pressure in one part of the globe, perhaps provoked by a butterfly flapping its wings, may be amplified through the system to produce hurricanes in another distant part of the globe. Self-reinforcing circles of storms or heat waves are often quite apparent. Because of this, it is impossible to make long-term weather forecasts. But even though we can say nothing about specific long-term weather patterns, we know that they will be similar to those experienced before. We know that these weather patterns are bounded in the sense that some patterns are not allowed by the system in some areas. We do not get snowstorms in the Sahara or heat waves in the Arctic, for example.

Chaotic behaviour, driven by nonlinear feedback, has also been demonstrated in gasses, chemical reactions, the movement of a driven pendulum, population changes and many more phenomena in nature.[2] An Institute has been set up in Santa Fe in California to promote multi-discipline research into complex systems, including economic systems. Newspapers report that some major securities houses are studying the behaviour of stock and foreign exchange markets in terms of chaos models. There is some evidence that chaotic behaviour may indeed apply to these markets.[3]

Consider the two important properties of chaos – unpredictability and irregular patterns.

Inherent unpredictability

When a nonlinear feedback system is set up to be relatively slow moving and unresponsive, then it operates in a state of stable equilibrium in which its long-term behaviour is perfectly predictable. A business system in this state will generate stable paths of profit over time (constancy or regular cycles), unless it is disturbed by unforeseen changes in the environment. It will have stable relationships with agents in its environment and the sequences of choices it makes will be predictable. There will be stable equilibrium in the sense that long-term behaviour is perfectly predictable and in the sense that it takes significant change to move the system away from these patterns of behaviour. Typical examples of business feedback systems operating in this stable state were to be found in companies operating in the traditional industries of northern England and the North Eastern States of the USA before the competitive onslaughts of the 1970s and 1980s.

If the same feedback system is made to be highly sensitive then it operates in a state of explosive equilibrium in which it will eventually disintegrate. This too is equilibrium in the sense that the long-term behaviour is perfectly predictable and in the sense that once in this pattern it takes a significant change to move the system out of it. We can find examples of business feedback systems in this state in some companies in the fast growing electronics industries – Apple seems to exhibit this kind of behaviour.

But if the system is given a level of sensitivity between those that generate stable and unstable equilibria, its specific behaviour or performance becomes random over the long term – but random within predictable limits. In this sense it is bounded instability. It is this that is part of the astonishing discovery made about nonlinear dynamics, for we have absolutely fixed feedback rules generating increasingly complicated time paths, culminating in one that is random within fixed limits, before exploding into instability.

When the system operates in this border area, it is highly sensitive to small changes in its environment. It uses positive feedback and operates in a manner that amplifies tiny fluctuations or disturbances throughout the system, leading to completely different, inherently unpredictable forms of behaviour. Because tiny changes can alter the behaviour of the system so completely, in effect its long-term development depends upon chance. That long-term behaviour is characterised by self-reinforcing virtuous and vicious circles. Through positive amplifying feedback, through self-reinforcing virtuous and vicious circles, the system plays a part in its own future and the rest depends upon tiny changes in its environments and hence upon chance. The long-term future of a system operating in the border area of bounded instability unfolds in a manner dependent upon the detail of what it does and what the systems constituting its environment do. Clear-cut connections between cause and effect are lost in the unpredictable unfolding of events. Sensitive dependence on small changes means that chance plays a significant part in what happens to the system. But it also means that what an individual component of a system does can also have a profound effect on the future of the whole system.

Once a business is in the area of bounded instability, then even if nothing in the environment changes and nothing in the decision making process itself changes, performance will move over time in a random, inherently unpredictable manner within certain limits. If relationships with the environment are in the area of bounded instability then patterns in those relationships will develop over the long term in a random, inherently unpredictable manner. If the decision making loop is operating in the area of bounded instability, then specific choices in a sequence will be random and inherently unpredictable over the long-term.

Furthermore, if tiny changes in the environment lead to tiny changes in the performance, relationships, and choices of one time period, the long-term path of performance, relationships and choices will be completely different from what they would have been without that change. The structure of the system and the act of repeatedly feeding

65

back into it have the effect of escalating tiny changes into completely different time paths in performance, relationships and choices.

The important point to make about this area of bounded instability is this:

- It is totally impossible to forecast the specific long-term behaviour of the system.

- It is possible to forecast the conditions in which chaos will occur, provided that we can identify the precise form of the feedback rule driving the system. This is because the rules driving the feedback loops are precise, with a fixed structure, and they generate behaviour which passes through absolutely fixed stages from stable time paths through cycles to chaos, within which there are areas of stability, until it finally emerges into explosive instability.

- It is also possible to forecast the short-term development of the system because it takes time for small changes to escalate.

But even when we have identified the precise form of the rule it is totally impossible to forecast long-term behaviour when the dynamics are chaotic. It is not just that the forecasting accuracy declines, it is completely impossible, even in principle, to predict specific outcomes.

There is not just one future to which the system moves as the result of some external cause. Instead, there are very many possible futures and the one which emerges will depend upon the precise detail of what the system does and what the systems constituting its environments do. There is no point in trying to simulate this future because you would have to know all this precise detail in advance to get anywhere near the future which will emerge. It is impossible to obtain the degree of detailed knowledge needed to specify the behaviour of the system in advance. Simulation and scenario building have no predictive power. The only scenario of any use is the one which will emerge in real time and to identify it you have to wait and see what happens. It may be useful to use simulation and scenarios to practice or learn in advance how to handle general kinds of situations that might arise, but such an exercise is hypothetical practice – the real situation will be different.

The key consequence of chaotic behaviour is that the link between cause and effect is lost in the unfolding of detailed events. It will often be impossible to look back and link causes with subsequent effects. Events emerge. Chance plays an important part in the unfolding behaviour of the system. But so does the detail of the behaviour of the system itself and that of actors within the system.

If we think about the difficulties in accounting for the superior performance of Japanese companies and for the decline in British and American heavy industries, we can see how this applies to the world of business. After years of research and libraries of books published on these subjects, there are still no universally accepted causal links to account for these phenomena. We still have only widely conflicting explanations.

Now if this inherent unpredictability over the long term and this fuzzy connection between cause and effect, were the only properties of chaos and we were to find that businesses have chaotic dynamics, then we would have real trouble in coping. But this is not all there is to chaos. The second important property of chaos is what has been referred to as a 'hidden' pattern.

Irregular patterns

Chaos is not simply random unstable behaviour alone because the instability is bounded – there are limits outside of which the time path does not move, but within which behaviour is random. Chaos is not runaway, explosive instability because it is constrained by the structure of the rule generating it. As a consequence chaotic behaviour has an overall, qualitative pattern to it, within which specific outcomes are random. This distinction is that which exists between a category and the variety of individual items and events within that category. For example, there is a category we call snowflakes, but within that category each individual snowflake pattern is different. Each snowflake is clearly recognisable as such, but it is also different from all others because it is a record of its history as it fell to the earth. As it did so, tiny differences in its exposure to temperature and air impurities, compared to nearby snowflakes, were amplified into different patterns.

When a feedback system generates stable equilibrium behaviour there is no fundamental distinction between a category and the individuals within that category. All individual items and events within the category are exactly the same – at equilibrium they are all adapted to the same environment in the same way. In a sense there are no individuals.

67

Nothing is added to our understanding by distinguishing between a category and the individuals which constitute it. The same point applies to explosive instability. But when behaviour is chaotic, there is an important distinction between a category and the individuals constituting it. The individuals are not all the same, they are only similar enough to warrant inclusion in the category. We can then talk about history repeating itself and yet always being different.

To see how this relates to the world of business, consider how competitive advantage is built up in certain geographic locations. Common patterns, at a qualitative level, can be detected in the development of businesses around certain educational institutions. Research centres of excellence in micro electronics and information technology at Stanford and Berkeley, together with the availability of skilled labour, played an important part in the development of Silicon valley in California. The availability of advanced technology made this an attractive location for electronics manufacturers in the early stages of that industry's development. These businesses in turn attracted component suppliers and other support companies. What we can observe is a feedback process through which a particular constellation of industries is built up to provide a particular set of competitive advantages.

A similar process can be observed around Cambridge in the UK. Once again a research centre of excellence has played an important part in the initial attraction of electronics and information technology firms. Feedback connections attracted others to establish a whole new industrial area. Similar developments are to be observed between Reading and Bristol, for similar reasons. But the specific composition of the industries which have grown up around San Francisco, around Cambridge and between Reading and Bristol are quite different. For example, neither of the two UK areas contain silicon chip manufacturers.

Similar patterns of geographic development in fashion clothing and shoes can be observed in northern Italy around Milan. The process is the same. Some initial advantage attracts a small cluster of companies. Through feedback, support industries are attracted and so the pattern develops. We can detect and recognise these patterns of geographic economic development, but their specific form is unpredictable, depending to a significant extent on chance. Failed attempt after failed attempt by governments artificially to establish such geographic concentrations through planned industrial policies, attests to this unpredictability. We can recognise geographical patterns of economic development as we become involved in them, but we cannot predict how these patterns will evolve in specific terms. Nor can we establish direct links to what causes them. The pattern that emerges depends on many escalating small events.

The 'hidden' pattern is therefore the essential feature of the category. It is the self-similarity of the individuals. We conclude that individuals belong to a category by looking for the similarity. We identify the features the individuals have in common, using some judgemental criteria to decide whether an individual is similar enough to be included in the category. But we could look at it another way. The criteria could relate to the degree of dissimilarity or irregularity. We would then only include individuals in the category if there was a constant degree of irregularity between them – if they did not deviate by more than a fixed limit. In chaotic patterns the individuals are never exactly the same but they are all regularly irregular. The key point is that the 'hidden' patterns or category features are qualitative, not quantitative. They are recognisable even if we cannot pin them down. For example, we are often able to recognise individuals as belonging to the same family, even though we cannot specify exactly what the common features are that allow us to draw this conclusion.

Chaotic behaviour can take the form of changing shapes in space over time, changing sequences of individual events over time or changing groupings of related events over time. Each individual shape or event will be different in specific terms; they will be random and unpredictable in specific terms. But if they are generated by the same feedback rules, they will share category features taking a general qualitative or family resemblance form. The category features cannot be rigidly defined: they are not hard and fast, clear-cut sets of common features. Perhaps the best description of these features is family resemblance, associativeness and relatedness which is hard to pin down but which we can recognise. The 'hidden' pattern is regular irregularity.

Non-equilibrium

This state of bounded instability is a non-equilibrium one, because behaviour patterns are in constant flux. The system does not continuously display constant paths or regular cycles on the one hand, or predictably explosive paths of unstable equilibrium on the other. Instead, tiny changes may push the system from regularity into random paths (within boundaries) and further tiny changes could push it back to regularity again. Behaviour is complex and unstable, but not explosively so – there are constraints or boundaries provided by the structure of the feedback mechanism itself. The amplifying nature of the structure itself generates bounded instability even in the absence of environmental change. In other words, instability comes from within the system itself, not simply from the environment as it does when the system operates in the area of stable equilibrium. Bounded instability takes the form of completely unpredictable specific events, but always within general, qualitative, recognisable irregular patterns.

CHAOS AND BUSINESS SUCCESS?

Since a business is a complex set of nonlinear feedback mechanisms, it must be capable of operating in the chaos border area of unbounded instability. The far-from-equilibrium choice must be open to it. The real question is whether such behaviour has anything to do with success.

The current view is that a successful business is really a system operating in stable equilibrium demonstrating instability only because it is continually disturbed by random shocks from its environment. Such instability is overcome by swift reaction to adapt to the change – in other words, negative feedback. If this is true then we would not expect to find successful managers intentionally employing positive feedback. Success would not be characterised by escalation of small changes, by self-reinforcing virtuous and vicious circles. Negative feedback would remove them, so restoring stability. The dynamic of success in this view is provided by the drive to the stability of adaptive equilibrium.

Modern dynamics suggests an alternative view of the dynamics of success. This is that success, where that means continual innovation, will come from operating in the chaos border area. So, what signs would we look for to test this view for a business? The signs of chaos are:

- escalating small changes;

- self-reinforcing virtuous and vicious circles;

- the application of amplifying, positive feedback; and

- the non equilibrium behaviour of continually unfolding, unpredictable patterns of behaviour which are nevertheless familiar in a qualitative, irregular sense.

If we detect these signs in the behaviour of successful companies, if we find that creative managers intentionally apply positive feedback, then this will be strong evidence that the dynamics of success are chaotic.

Recognising chaos

It should be stressed, at this point, that we would describe the dynamics of a particular business as chaotic if we could point to behaviour on the part of its managers that has amplifying, escalating, self-reinforcing, unpredictable effects over the long term. We would not describe the dynamics as chaotic if we observe simply that there is no order at all; if we observe that managers are running from one short-term crisis to another, failing to deliver product on time to the right quality, at the right cost. We would not describe the dynamics as chaotic by simply observing that there is no clear hierarchy, no clear job definitions, everyone doing anything that came into their heads. That would be total confusion, a complete mess, which is not what we mean by chaos in its scientific sense.

It would not be possible to walk into a company and immediately observe chaos in its scientific sense. What we would see in a company with chaotic dynamics is visible order, tight short interval controls, consistent delivery to quality, time and cost targets. These would all be secured through damping forms of control, through negative feedback applied to the short-term consequence of events and actions.

Chaotic dynamics would be evidenced by escalation of small changes and self-reinforcing virtuous and vicious circles in the manner in which managers dealt with events and actions having long-term consequences. It would be perfectly consistent to observe managers amplifying some changes, while at the same time damping the consequences of others. Successful managers do use different forms of control. When they are dealing with the predictable short-term consequences of changes to the current form of the existing business, they apply damping forms of control. When they deal with new developments having highly uncertain long-term consequences, they may well apply amplifying forms of control. If chaos applies to business, it will apply to the manner in which managers deal with issues having long-term consequences.

- Do managers intentionally use amplifying feedback to achieve long-term success?

- Do small changes escalate over the long term?

- Do successful businesses provoke self-reinforcing circles?

- What evidence is there that successful businesses operate in a non-equilibrium state?

That chaos has much to do with success can be seen quite clearly, I believe, if we consider the amplifying, non-equilibrium nature of successful relationships between an organisation and its environment. That chaos has much to do with success can also be seen by considering the nature of the decision making or control processes appropriate for conditions of great uncertainty. It will be argued in the next section that in both cases managers intentionally use amplifying feedback loops and that the consequence is clearly observable escalation of small changes and the development of self-reinforcing virtuous and vicious circles.

Feedback and the environment

Consider first the relationships that successful managers have with the people who constitute the environment of their business. The stable equilibrium mindset includes the unquestioned assumption that the requirements of customers are independently determined by forces outside the influence of the managers responding to them. The assumption is that customers have requirements – discovered through market research, through listening to them, through making trial offerings and seeing how they respond. On this assumption, the successful company offers what is closest to customer requirement. When the requirement changes, the offering must be changed to sustain adaptive equilibrium if the company is to be a continuing success. And the competitor making the most adapted offerings is the one that will survive.

But this whole view ignores the feedback nature of the relationships between managers and the people who are their customers, competitors, suppliers and government regulators of one kind or another. These relationships are clearly of a feedback nature. When managers in one organisation take some action, other managers in other organisations or individual customers respond in some way. Those responses lead to further actions on the part of the first set of managers and so it goes on. For example, one company cuts its prices, a competitor responds by cutting its prices. The first cuts prices further and other competitors join in. A self-reinforcing price war ensues. One action feeds into another, which in turn feeds back into the first in a loop over time. Consider then some key aspects of the feedback nature of relationships with the environment.

Managers create, or at the very least, they shape the requirements of their customers through the product offerings they make.

Creating and shaping customer requirements

Managers frequently create customer perceptions and thus customer requirements. If this was not possible there would be no point in advertising. Sony created a requirement for personal hi fi systems through its Walkman offering. Manufacturers and operators have created requirements for portable telephones. Sony and Matsushita created the requirement for video recorders. And so one may go on. This is not a picture of managers clearly identifying what customers want and then providing it. It is a picture of managers making an offering, customers responding to that offering, managers responding to the response and so on through time. The reader may argue that all those requirements were already there, lurking about waiting to be satisfied. But even if this is so, there can be little doubt that managers at least shape those requirements. The requirement for personal hi fi's, portable telephones and video recorders did not exist in clearly defined forms waiting for the technology to be available. The offerings that were made, defined the shape of the requirement.

This shaping activity can be seen quite clearly in other areas of business activity. When a management consultant and client begin to talk about a possible assignment, normally the client does not have a completely clear-cut idea of the services required from the consultant.

The consultant helps to shape that requirement through discussion, that is, feedback. And it does not matter that the consultant is a one man band while the client is a major corporation. The consultant shapes the requirement in the same way.

The same point applies to companies supplying information systems to their clients. Generally speaking, the client does not have a completely specified system in mind. Mostly, the client does not know exactly, or often even vaguely, what he or she wants. The supplier plays a considerable role in shaping the requirement.

These creating and shaping activities of managers in effect set up a feedback loop between the offerings they make and the customers' requirements. The offering itself creates or modifies the requirement. And the requirement then impacts on subsequent offerings. This is not that one way relationship implied by the idea of a business adapting to its environment. Instead it is an amplifying feedback loop. Creative managers seize on small differences in customer requirements and perceptions to build significant differentiators for their products. Customers may respond to this by switching from other product offerings, leading to a virtuous circle. Or, as once happened to Coca Cola, a small change in ingredients may lead to switches away and therefore vicious circles.

And the loops are complex, because they do not run simply from a company to its customers. There is strong feedback interaction between such a company and its competitors. Competitors respond to each others' offerings, leading in turn to further responses. Suppliers to these competitors will also exert a shaping influence on the latters' product offerings, as will legal and regulatory requirements placed on them by yet other organisations.

Copying and spreading loops

There is another important feedback loop we need to take account of to get nearer to a more realistic model of business behaviour. The requirements of customers are linked to the responses they make through the effects of copying and spreading. Customers do not have given requirements quite independent of the manner in which they have previously responded, or the manner in which other customers are responding. In other words, the history of previous responses is incorporated into current responses. For example, customers have requirements for washing machines. The more they satisfy this requirement, the less the customer population wants additional units. So, demand today feeds back into demand tomorrow.

We also know that customers discover that they have requirements because they see other people with the product offering. We know that this leads to a spreading effect that may easily become cumulative and self-reinforcing. For example, the more people buy IBM personal computers, the more software becomes available, making it more attractive for others to buy IBM computers. If VHS video recorders become slightly more popular than Betamax, this will encourage film makers to provide more films in the VHS format. This will increase the incentive for others to buy VHS rather than Betamax. What we have here is amplifying feedback leading to self-reinforcing virtuous circles for some and vicious circles for others.

So, managers are intentionally shaping customer requirements through the offerings they make and this feeds back into customer responses and hence profitability each time the business moves around its profit feedback loop. Managers are intentionally using the copying and spreading effects through which responses to product offerings feed back into other customers' requirements and responses and hence into the profit feedback loop.

Adaptation loses its meaning

This intentional use of amplifying feedback loops connecting a business to its environments has extremely important consequences. It means that small changes can escalate and self-reinforcing virtuous and vicious circles can be triggered off. This leads to a consequence of great importance to the mental models we use when we design and control our actions. The idea of managers adapting to the environment loses its meaning, as does that of success as some form of stable equilibrium. When managers shape customer requirements, when they take steps to use the copying and spreading effects of customer behaviour, they are not adapting to a given environment. They are partially creating their own environment and getting the customers to adapt to them. It becomes rather difficult to say who is adapting to whom and this applies as much to a small business as it does to a large one; it simply applies over a smaller area in the case of a small company. In these circumstances what we find is not stable equilibrium but companies intentionally seeking to be drawn into self-reinforcing virtuous circles and sometimes unavoidably drawn into vicious ones.

> The video technology of Sony's Betamax exhibits market self-reinforcement in the sense that increased prevalence on the market encourages video outlets to stock more film titles in Betamax; there are coordination benefits to new purchasers of Betamax that increase with its market share. If Betamax and its rival VHS compete, a small lead in market share gained by one of the technologies may enhance its competitive position and help it further increase its lead. There is positive feedback. If both systems start out at the same time, market shares may fluctuate at the outset, as external circumstances and 'luck' change, and as backers manoeuvre for advantage. And if the self-reinforcing mechanism is strong enough, eventually one of the two technologies may accumulate enough advantage to take 100 per cent of the market. Notice however we cannot say in advance which one this will be. ... If one technology is inherently 'better' than the other ...but has 'bad luck' in gaining early adherents, the eventual outcome may not be of maximum possible benefit. (In fact, industry specialists claim that the actual loser in the video contest, Betamax, is technically superior to VHS.) ... Once a 'solution' is reached, it is difficult to exit from. In the video case, the dominant system's accrued advantage makes it difficult for the loser to break into the market again.[4]

Since, in the rapidly changing environments so common today, the most successful companies are those that keep innovating, success will not be found by adapting to the environment or establishing stable equilibrium positions. Adapting means finding out what the *definitely* existing requirements of customers are and then meeting those requirements as closely as possible. Innovation means creating and shaping requirements, positively using copying and spreading effects, in a continually amplifying feedback loop. The stable equilibrium of complete adaptation cannot be success in most of today's markets. Success also cannot be the unstable equilibrium of isolation from the environment. Success then lies in a non-equilibrium state between two equilibria; a state characterised by amplifying feedback with the escalation of small changes and the presence of self-reinforcing vicious and virtuous circles. Success requires operation in the border area of bounded instability generated by feedback relationships with the environment.

Feedback and the control system

This conclusion, that the dynamics of success are chaotic, is strengthened when we consider the business control system itself, its decision making process. Control systems are feedback loops in which one outcome triggers actions that yield further outcomes. When it comes to designing their control systems, that is, the organisational structures, information systems, management styles, processes and procedures of decision making, all businesses are powerfully pulled in two, fundamentally different, directions.

On the one hand efficiency requires task division, market segmentation and production process separation in geographic and other terms. Efficiency is secured through breaking things up into components, through some form of fragmentation. These efficiency requirements can only be met if individuals and organisational sub-units are motivated by satisfying their individual goals. These efficiency requirements lead to fragmenting cultures, dispersed power and informal channels of communication. All these efficiency factors pull an organisation and its control systems towards disintegration: we can think of this as a form of unstable explosive equilibrium. We can see this pull appearing in practice as companies divide management functions in greater and greater detail, as they split the organisation up into more and more decentralised business units. The more this decentralisation proceeds, the harder it becomes to maintain control and hold the organisation together.

To avoid this pull to disintegration, all businesses are also pulled to a state in which tasks are integrated, overlaps in market segments and production processes managed, group goals stressed above individual ones, power concentrated, communication and procedures are formalised and strongly shared cultures established. As a company moves in this direction it develops more and more rigid structures, rules, procedures and systems. It develops cohesion, strongly shared cultures and increasingly concentrated power. Organisations continuing to develop their control systems in this direction eventually ossify. This is a very stable equilibrium position, but one which makes it impossible for the organisation to cope with rapid change. These consequences are easy to observe as organisations proceed further and further down the road to centralisation.

So, one powerful set of forces pulls every business control system towards a stable equilibrium of ossification and another powerful set of forces pulls it towards an explosively unstable equilibrium of disintegration. Success lies between these states, where the organisation continually alters aspects of its control system to avoid attraction to either disintegration or ossification. For this reason we observe all business organisations on what seems to be a perpetual merry-go-round between centralisation and decentralisation. Once again, success lies in a non-equilibrium situation between stable and unstable equilibria. And for a nonlinear feedback system that is a chaos border area.

Success in control terms lies in a state of bounded instability. Successful control systems combine aspects of stability and instability, and use both negative and positive feedback. Short interval control is the application of negative feedback as we saw in a previous section. But when they control, managers also use amplifying behaviour. When they are confronted by ambiguous issues with potentially significant but unclear long-term consequences, they form coalitions to secure attention for those issues. They use the political tools of persuasion, negotiation and discussion to spread, or amplify, new ideas through the organisation. A small change, in the form of a dimly perceived new issue on the part of one or two managers, can escalate up into the undertaking of a major new activity by the company. Once embarked upon, the build up of that new activity can become either a virtuous or a vicious circle.

SUCCESS LIES IN CHAOS – BOUNDED INSTABILITY IS FUNDAMENTAL

To summarise, consider the key points of a far-from-equilibrium management mindset. Businesses are feedback systems because every performance indicator is interconnected with every other in some way and they are all subject to time lags. Every performance indicator, therefore, feeds back into a relationship connecting it to its own future values. For example, cash and profit are ploughed back into the business to yield further cash and profit flows. What happened yesterday affects what happens today and that affects what happens tomorrow. The links between performance now and performance tomorrow are provided by the decision making process of the company and by the relationships it has with other organisations and people in its environments. And each of these links is itself a set of feedback mechanisms. The more responsive the decision making process and the more responsive the relationships with the environment, the more sensitive is the whole set of feedback mechanisms, the faster the business moves around the loops. And these feedback mechanisms are nonlinear because their operation is constrained by capacity, finance, skills, and fundamental economic laws of demand, diminishing returns and economies of scale.

We have always thought that such systems have a choice between two states of behaviour. They can either behave in a stable orderly manner, which the use of negative feedback can secure. Or they can operate in a much higher state of sensitivity where feedback becomes positive. The result is explosive instability. Both are equilibrium states. The strong forces of negative feedback keep the system stable, or the strong forces of positive feedback lead it to disintegrate. Given this choice, a business system can only be successful if it is sustained in stable equilibrium in which it adapts to its environment. If we observe that a business develops in an unstable, irregular manner we have to conclude that this is because its managers are incompetently operating the control systems or they are unavoidably subjected to random shocks from the environment to which they are unable to react fast enough.

Scientists, however, have discovered that there is a third choice open to such a nonlinear feedback system: that of behaviour which is bounded instability. They have discovered that as the sensitivity of a nonlinear feedback system is increased it moves from stable equilibrium patterns of behaviour (which may be highly complex), through a phase of bounded instability, before it becomes explosively unstable. That phase of bounded instability has been named chaos. Chaotic behaviour is random and hence unpredictable at the specific or individual level. The particular behaviour that emerges is highly sensitive to small changes and hence depends to some extent upon chance. But this is not explosive instability because it is constrained. And because it is constrained it always displays a pattern of category features, a kind of qualitative family resemblance. In this state the system uses positive feedback, albeit in a constrained manner.

Since a business is a system driven by nonlinear feedback mechanisms it must be capable of all three forms of behaviour. The key question is, which of these forms is necessary for the innovative business? And the answer is that an innovative business will always operate in the chaos area. The grounds for saying this are as follows:

- The nature of relationships with the environment. Businesses are systems that interact with each other: they form each others' environments. They do not simply adapt but creatively interact with each other. Their relationships with each other are clearly of a feedback nature and we observe that small changes escalate and self-reinforcing virtuous and vicious circles appear. The feedback mechanism which is relationship with the environment is therefore operating in chaos when successful.

- The nature of business control systems. These too are feedback mechanisms. Those that heavily emphasise integration all the time tend towards a form of ossification in which they cannot handle rapid change. Control systems that emphasise division all the time tend to disintegrate. Successful control systems display features of both integration and division; they occupy a difficult to maintain position between two equilibria. And for nonlinear feedback mechanisms this area between two equilibria is chaos.

Managers intentionally use amplifying feedback both in relation to their environments and in their internal political activities. The results we observe are the signs of chaos – escalation and self-reinforcing virtuous and vicious circles.

HOW A NEW MINDSET WILL LEAD MANAGERS TO THINK AND ACT IN A DIFFERENT WAY

The science of dynamic system complexity provides a fundamentally different mental model with which to interpret business behaviour and design innovative management actions. Unlike today's most prominent mental models, it does not focus simply on stability, consistency and cohesion as the prerequisites of business success. Because it is built upon the continuing interactive feedback involved in real competitive games, it provides a more realistic insight into the dynamics of that creatively unfolding game. It explicitly recognises the unstable, disorderly aspects of that game. It accounts for the escalation of small changes and the self-reinforcing virtuous and vicious circles generated by that game. When managers design their actions with such a mental model, they will not confuse success with simple stability. They will not seek to impose the order of plans and visions in conditions which make it impossible for those plans and visions to contribute to effective long-term control. They will consequently not engage in the curious and contradictory behaviour described in Chapter 2. Instead, they will seek to operate in conditions of bounded instability. They will seek to interact creatively with the other people who constitute the environment of their business.

The conclusion we reach, then, is that excellent companies will operate in a state in which instability is fundamental to success. Instability is not just due to ignorance or incompetence, it is a fundamental property of successful business systems. Successful managers positively use constrained instability to provoke innovation. The next chapter explores how business systems use this instability to innovate – how they create order out of chaos.

REFERENCES

1. Peters, T & Waterman, R H (1982) *In Search of Excellence*, Harper & Rowe, New York.

2. Gleick, J (1987) *Chaos: Making a New Science*, Heinemann, New York.

3. Shenkman, J & Le Baron, B (1989) 'Nonlinear Dynamics and Stock Returns', Journal of Business, vol. 62, no. 3.

    Hsieh, D (1989) 'Testing for Nonlinear Dependence in Daily Foreign Exchange Returns', Journal of Business, vol. 62, no. 3.

4. Arthur, W B (1988) 'Self-Reinforcing Mechanisms in Economics', in P W Anderson, K J Arrow & D Pines (eds), *The Economy as a Complex Evolving System*, Addison-Wesley, Menlo Park, Ca.

4

Creativity and Destruction: Spontaneity and Unpredictability

The last chapter discussed how well defined, orderly systems could generate chaotic behaviour. It also considered the relationship between this chaotic behaviour and continuing innovation. It concluded that a successful business organisation is one that operates in the chaos border area. This chapter considers other scientific discoveries about the behaviour of dynamic systems. These discoveries shed light on how such systems produce new order from chaos. The concern here is with the relationship between chaos and the process of creativity.

CHAOS AND CONTINUING CREATIVITY

In today's rapidly changing environment, success is reaped by those businesses that continually innovate. Success requires continual creativity that the business itself must initiate. How do stable systems meet this requirement?

When a business is in a state of stable equilibrium, it operates in a predictable manner, making it possible to control behaviour with pre-programmed rules, procedures, objectives, plans, shared perceptions, attitudes and cultures. Analytical techniques can be applied to large quantities of information to yield accurate solutions to problems. The whole point is to keep the system doing the same thing over and over again until some change in the environment makes it necessary to make a corresponding and matching internal change – control takes the form of damping, negative feedback. Effective acts in this context are those that anticipate environmental changes. Failing that, effective acts are those that develop a rapid and appropriate response to an unforeseen change, the random shock. Effectiveness is adaptive proaction and rapid reaction where that fails.

And because the system is stable, creativity in the sense of doing something new is very difficult. It will require substantial change in structures, rules, procedures and plans every time a significant random shock is encountered. Substantial changes to structures, rules and procedures are very difficult to make because they require altering stable relationships between people, work patterns, attitudes, perceptions and cultures. When systems are close to adaptive equilibrium, it takes major internal change to be creative, or even to cope with major random shocks from the environment.

But when a system is far-from-equilibrium in the chaos area of bounded instability, it is much easier for its behaviour to change. In this state, perceptions, attitudes and cultures are not strongly shared. Here, clear rules, and procedures, objectives and plans cannot be established in advance to deal with the long term because of the problem of unpredictability. In chaos small changes can easily escalate into major changes of behaviour. The bounded instability of contention makes the positive contribution of shattering old perceptions and attitudes and preventing rigid, uniform cultures from developing. Without this, the new cannot emerge. In the language of the scientists, chaos breaks symmetries and this is an essential part of the emergence of new order in systems driven by nonlinear feedback mechanisms.

Destruction and creativity are closely related to each other and continuing creativity requires continuing destruction. This is by no means a new idea in economics or business. Back in the 1930s, the economist Schumpeter stressed that a firm must practice 'creative destruction' on itself to sustain competitive advantage. It must destroy its old advantages by creating new ones and if it does not, some rival will.

What does constitute a new discovery is how nonlinear feedback systems develop new order out of chaos. Take the laser beam. When a hot solid or gas is close to thermodynamic equilibrium, each atom emits light randomly and independently. As a result the gas or solid behaves like an ordinary lamp, with its light extending over only a few metres – the beams of light from the atoms combine to form an incoherent jumble of light waves. The system can be driven away from equilibrium by further heating the solid or gas, putting an excessive number of the atoms into excited states. Their behaviour is chaotic. During this chaos, a critical point is reached and the atoms suddenly organise themselves on a global scale to display cooperative behaviour of a very precise kind. All the atoms emit waves of light that are exactly in phase. The result is a coherent ray of light stretching over very long distances. This phenomenon is not predictable from the laws of physics.

Another example of spontaneous self-organisation in a system driven far-from-equilibrium occurs when a horizontal layer of fluid is heated from below. The warm liquid at the bottom rises. At low temperatures the warm fluid rises to the top in an orderly manner. But when the temperature is raised further the liquid becomes unstable and starts to convect. When the temperature at the bottom of the layer of fluid reaches a critical point, the convecting liquid adopts a highly orderly and stable pattern, organizing itself into distinctive rolls with a hexagonal cell structure. Further heating may lead to other transitions including the onset of chaos. The detailed arrangement of the convection cells cannot be predicted and the experimenter has no control over whether a given part of the fluid will end up in a clockwise or anticlockwise rotating cell.

At each point of transition, systems driven far-from-equilibrium move through patterns of instability in which previous symmetry or order is broken, thus confronting the system with choices at critical points. Through a process of spontaneous self-organisation, a form of communication and cooperation between the components of the system, new order may be produced. The important point is that such phase transitions do not necessarily have predictable outcomes – the possibility is there in some cases for the system to make choices that produce new and unexpected behaviour. Chance may be involved in moving from one state to another and this is definitely not a possibility in near-to-equilibrium states, where the outcome is predictable. New order emerges through a process in which the components of the system spontaneously self organise at critical points in the system's development to produce an unpredictable new order.

In chaos then, creativity is a potentially ongoing process that is internally generated in a spontaneous manner. It is not proaction or reaction to environmental change. It is continuing interaction with other systems in the environment. It has to do with a system playing a part in its own future, with partly creating its own environment.

But what does this have to do with a successful business? First, instability does play a major role in generating new perspectives and innovations. Second, we can observe exactly the same process as that described above for nature's systems, when managers in a business handle open-ended strategic issues. Strategic management in practice is a process of spontaneous self-organisation that may produce the new order of innovation and new strategic direction.

MANAGERS PROVOKE INSTABILITY

Initially some managers are rather startled by the idea that instability plays a vitally important destructive role in continuing creativity; that innovations arise unpredictably from some kind of centrally uncontrolled spontaneous process. But the idea is not that startling at all. Managers frequently reorganise the structures of their companies. They also frequently justify such reorganisations in the following terms. 'This reorganisation will change relationships between people; it will alter work patterns; and it will convey strong messages that things are going to be different.' Such reorganisations are purposely destabilising and the explicit intention is to shatter existing patterns of attitudes, personal relationships, and work. It is using instability to bring about change – and it quite clearly implies some reliance on self-organisation. If the new organisation could set out quite unambiguously what people are now to do and ensure that they did it, there would be no need to talk about changing attitudes and relationships or sending messages. The idea of doing these things is to create conditions in which people will do things differently in a spontaneous manner.

Further evidence that managers intentionally provoke instability in order to alter behaviour patterns and so encourage spontaneous creativity is provided by a study carried out by Ikujiro Nonaka.[1] His survey of Japanese companies shows how they use chaos for self renewal. Consider some quotes:

> Honda is well known for a culture in which confrontation is encouraged among employees regardless of rank. Kawashima, the former President, has been quoted as saying, 'I decided to step down as president because the employees began agreeing with me 70 per cent of the time.' ....
>
> Countercultures are formed by hiring new employees with diverse specialities and introducing new employees through mid-career

employment. The Copier Division of Canon Inc., for example, has many employees who joined the company through mid-way hiring. It is necessary to keep hiring these people until a certain critical mass is reached so that they will be able to oppose the existing values. At Honda, mid-way hiring is practised in order to 'give impact to existing persons and organization through the introduction of new blood'. Moreover, it is customarily done deliberately every two or three years instead of employing a fixed number each year. ....

Canon's President Kaku is quoted as saying:

> A company begins to decline as soon as one thinks it has become a premier company. There are two things which the top management must keep in mind in order to guarantee the continuing existence of the company. The first task of top management is to create a vision that gives meaning to the employees' jobs. The second task is to constantly convey a sense of crisis to their employees.

Chaos is a prerequisite for continuing interactive creation and innovation. Implicitly at least, managers recognise this when they intentionally introduce destabilising changes in order to break down existing behaviour patterns and provoke new ones. And they do this without knowing exactly what new patterns they are trying to provoke. Successful companies have chaotic dynamics because in this state:

- they do not carry on doing the same thing until environmental change forces them to do otherwise;

- they play a part in creating their own environments and their own futures;

- they are capable of playing nimble, highly interactive games with competitors and customers; games in which small changes escalate and virtuous and vicious circles appear.

HOW MANAGERS MANAGE A BUSINESS IN OPEN-ENDED SITUATIONS

If we observe how managers actually behave when confronted by open-ended changes, we can see that there is a rhythm to, or a number of phases in, that behaviour. Phases of this kind have been demonstrated in the relatively few studies so far made of political processes in business organisations.[2] These phases are depicted in Figure 4.1.

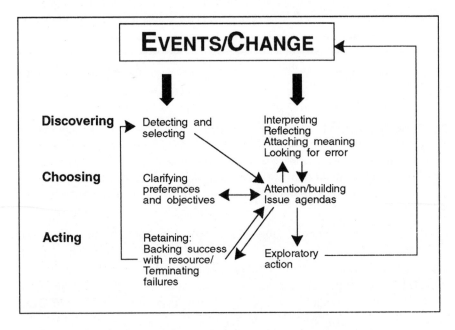

Figure 4.1 Dealing with open-ended issues

The behaviour depicted in Figure 4.1 is the discovering, choosing and acting that constitutes organisational learning and political interaction. Each phase in that behaviour is briefly summarised below.

Detecting and selecting open-ended issues

Open-ended change is typically the accumulating result of many small events and actions. And it is this kind of change with which strategic management is concerned. What is going on is unclear, ambiguous and confusing, with consequences that are unknowable. The key difficulty is to identify what the real issues, problems and opportunities are. The challenge is to find an appropriate and creative aspiration or objective. In these circumstances the organisation has no alternative but to rely on the initiative of individuals to notice and pursue some issue, aspiration or challenge. And in order to do this, those individuals have to rely on their experience-based intuition and ability to detect analogies between one set of ambiguous circumstances and another. This activity on the part of an individual is spontaneous and self-organising in the sense that no central authority can direct anyone to detect and select an open-ended issue for attention, simply because no one knows what it is until someone has detected it. You cannot instruct someone to 'have a good idea'.

The importance of this reliance on the spontaneous self-organisation of individuals intuitively to detect and select open-ended issues is most obvious in the case of well known individual entrepreneurs. For example, the history of Amstrad, since its foundation in the 1970s to the present time, is a story of the open-ended issues which its founder Alan Sugar detected and selected for attention. He noticed in the 1970s that plastic covers for record players would be much cheaper if made by an injection moulding rather than a vacuum forming process. This led to the creation of a lucrative product. He detected that most people did not want to go to the trouble of assembling a number of different hi fi units, but they liked the fashionable appearance of a hi fi set. So he created an all-in-one tower system consisting of one unit which looked like a number of different units. Sales of these low priced units ran into millions. He detected that potential customers for personal computers knew too little about them to be able to assemble a number of different units and load software onto them. So he created a low cost product which could be taken from the store, plugged in and used immediately.

Forming special interest groups and coalitions

And the birth of a strategy is no different in any other corporation. Some individual, at some level in the hierarchy, detects a potential issue and begins to push for organisational attention to be paid to that issue. What does differ between an organisation run by an all-powerful entrepreneur and others, is the complexity of the political process required to gain attention for an issue. At Amstrad an issue received organisational attention if Alan Sugar was persuaded to attend to it. In most organisations however, a more complex process of building special interest groups or coalitions around an issue is required before that issue can be said to have gained organisational attention. This political activity of building support for attention to some detected issue is also clearly self-organising and spontaneous in the sense that it is informal and not part of the normal rules and procedures. No one is centrally organising the factions and coalitions that form around detected issues.

The strategic issue agenda

Once an issue has gained sufficient support, in the sense that it is being discussed by those with sufficient power to do something about it, then that issue becomes part of the organisation's strategic issue agenda. This agenda is at the heart of strategic management. It is the focus of the organisational learning through which the business develops new strategic directions. It is a dynamic list of issues, aspirations and challenges that are on the list, not because they are written down, but because key groups of managers are attending to them. It is alive because managers are attending to it. It is dynamic because it is always changing in a manner that reflects what is being detected, how the pattern of political interplay is developing and what managers are learning. Issues arrive on the agenda; some are attended to, others drop off the list without ever being acted upon. Yet others are successfully enacted and others lead to actions that fail. Successful companies, creative companies, have live, active strategic issue agendas.

So at Amstrad in the mid 1980s we find large numbers of issues relating to different computer products, sourcing components in the Far East, manufacturing and assembly, setting up distribution channels in Europe, organisational structures and control systems, as well as many more.

When managers deal with the issues on their strategic agenda they are performing a real-time learning activity. There is no overall framework to which they can refer before they decide how to tackle an issue. Through discussion with each other and with customers, suppliers and even rivals they are discovering what objectives they should pursue and what actions might work. In this sense they are learning what to do as they progress the issue. They are in effect altering old mental models, existing company and industry recipes, and coming up with a new way of doing things. They are clarifying and discovering preferences, aspirations and objectives.

The communication which all of this involves is spontaneous in the sense that it is not directed by some central authority. The communication that occurs depends upon the individuals involved. And that depends upon the boundary conditions, or context, provided by individual personalities, the dynamic of their interaction with each other, and the time they have available, given all the other issues requiring attention.

When managers deal with the strategic issue agenda of their organisation, they are performing a vitally important destabilising function. Strategic issues, by definition, threaten existing work patterns, organisational structures and power positions. Strategic issues are about new, different ways of doing things and different things to do. One issue has to compete with other issues for attention and scarce resource. Progressing issues through discussion, conflict and dialogue is an activity that changes perceptions. This instability and confusion, or chaos, performs the function of shattering the existing order to make the new possible. Handling issues on the agenda, building support is an activity that amplifies this instability through the system. It is what scientists call *symmetry breaking* in nature's systems.

Critical points – consensus and commitment

Some issues on the agenda may be dealt with very quickly. Others may attract attention, continuous or periodic, for a very long time. How quickly an issue is dealt with depends upon the time required to reach enough consensus and commitment to proceed to action. It depends upon the course which the political and learning interaction takes. At some critical point, some external pressure, or some internal pressure arising from power, personality or group interaction, in effect forces a choice. The outcome on whether and how to proceed to action over the issue is unpredictable because it depends upon the context of power, personality and group dynamic. The result may or may not be some action.

The point about this consensus required to proceed to action is that it is temporary, fragile and related to a specific issue. When the group of managers turns to the next issue, consensus has to be established anew. In a dynamic organisation, one dealing with an active, ever-changing issue agenda, consensus will be the exception, not the norm. It requires continuing inputs of energy and attention to sustain consensus. It is what scientists call a *dissipative* structure.

Experimental action and feedback

Action will usually be experimental at first, so providing a vehicle for further learning. Amstrad first set up agents in France, Spain and Germany. Once this demonstrated realisable potential, subsidiary companies were established. Actors in the environment respond to the actions managers take in a company. Through that response, those environmental actors change the situation. Such changes are fed back into the learning loop of the company and lead to further learning and hence further action. The Amstrad operations in France, Spain and Germany all developed in different ways, and Amstrad learned from them. It used the more successful French model to redesign operations in Spain and Germany. Task forces are set up to carry out experimental actions such as the development of a new product. The operation of such task forces is a continuing political and learning process.

Legitimating and backing

A key point is the manner in which building and handling strategic issue agendas proceeds largely outside the formal structures and procedures of the organisation. But at various points in this largely spontaneous and self-organising process, the formal bodies and procedures are required to legitimate the choices being made and to allocate resources to the exploration of, and experimentation with, issues. The support and interest of the formal bodies in the organisation is vital to the effective building and progressing of strategic issues. But such bodies are essentially peripheral. They provide the boundaries within which the self-organising process of dealing with strategic issues occurs. As unclear open-ended issues proceed through learning and experimentation to emerge as potentially successful new strategies, the formal bodies of the organisation play a more prominent role. New strategies will only emerge if those bodies back potential success with sufficient resource to allow the new strategy to emerge.

Retained memory – the culture

Managers in a business come to share memories of what has worked and what has not worked in the past. In this way they build up a business philosophy for their company; they establish a company recipe and in common with other rivals they build industry recipes too. All of this is the same as developing a culture or a retained organisational memory. It is this which is often referred to as a 'vision'. But the important point is that this 'vision' is retrospective, not prospective.

An organisation's memory has a powerful effect on what issues will subsequently be detected and attended to. It constitutes the frame of reference within which managers interpret what to do next – and this retained memory provides yet another boundary around the instability of the political and learning processes through which strategic issues are handled. It is a boundary that has to be managed because it can easily become inappropriate to new circumstances. An essential part of the complex learning process required to handle strategic issues is the continual questioning of the organisation's retained memory.

For example, shortly after a speech in which Alan Sugar set out the Amstrad business philosophy of aggressive entrepreneurialism, he adopted a rather different approach:

> Ironically, Sugar delivered his City University speech just as Amstrad was in the process of abandoning crucial ingredients of its ultra-entrepreneurial, small business ethos. Few people realized it at the time, but in many ways the address set the seal on the first twenty years of Amstrad's existence. Indeed, Sugar had already sown some of the seeds which would grow into structures more appropriate for a large company.[3]

Successful managers do not cling to one business philosophy no matter what. They learn, they change their mindset to generate new ways of doing things.

The life cycle of an issue

The central part of the learning/political control and development loop described above is the strategic issue agenda. It is always changing and at any one time it will contain some vague issues around which intentions are many and half-formed. There will also be issues that have reached an advanced stage of clarification. There will be others where a consensus has formed and we can talk of shared intention around that issue.

Any one issue, therefore, tends to follow something of a life cycle. It starts life as a vague, half-formed issue and the principal tasks are to clarify it, identify objectives in relation to it, and build support for it. Here planning forms of control and development have no contribution to make. But if that issue is progressed, it eventually reaches a stage of clarity where objectives can be formed. At this point planning enters as the form to control project execution. If now the outcomes of actions taken to deal with the issue are predictable, then a fuller form of planning becomes possible for that project. Issues, the consensus required to do something about them, the objectives to achieve, all emerge from the learning activity. Having emerged, having been clarified, other forms of control and development then have a part to play. But this is planning around a major issue, not planning the future of the system as a whole.

PRINCIPAL FEATURES

What the above seven steps describe is a feedback control loop that operates in an amplifying manner within boundaries. It is political interaction and learning in real-time. It is control because behaviour is connected and constrained. The outcome emerges as the result of converging and emerging individual and sub-unit intentions. All of these steps have been identified by one piece of research or another. But, when we interpret them from a dynamic systems perspective, we are led to focus on two important features:

- the positive role of instability and unpredictability;

- the importance and nature of spontaneity and self-organisation.

The importance and positive role of instability and unpredictability

At the most visible level, that is, in the day-to-day conduct of their existing businesses, successful organisations display a stable, orderly face to their customers, competitors, suppliers, managers and employees. They deliver consistent quality, on time, at cost targets. The outside world sees an understandable organisational structure focused on market segments – customers and suppliers know who they are dealing with. Those within the organisation see well defined jobs within a clear hierarchy setting out reporting lines and responsibilities for the delivery of competitive products. They see orderly information and control systems yielding plans and targets that enable people to know what they are doing on a day-to-day basis. They are aware of their business philosophy – the recipe, or shared culture built upon previous experience of successfully working together. At the most visible level success is cohesion, harmony, regularity and order.

But a successful business operates on more than one level. In addition to the stable, damping control of the existing business, at the same time, successful businesses continually create new strategic directions. They re-package existing products and create new market segments. They identify new groups of customers, new distribution channels, new sources of supply, new approaches to manufacturing. They develop new products, new technologies, different forms of day-to-day control, different reward systems, new approaches to staff selection, training and development. And the key point is that operating at this level, where the new is created, involves behaviour that is diametrically opposed to the orderly conduct of the day-to-day business. This is because creating the new inevitably destroys the old. Almost every potential alteration in the nature or conduct of the existing business creates opportunities for some and threatens the existing work patterns, roles, positions or relative power of other individuals or organisational sub-units. Operating at the frontiers of the new is therefore inherently destabilising to the organisation.

Furthermore, the new can only arise in conditions of instability. The heart of creative strategic management lies in the ability of managers within an organisation continually to develop live, active strategic issue agendas. Such issues arise when individuals perceive some incongruity with what is currently going on; when they question the established recipes, cultures and business philosophies. A live strategic issue agenda depends upon people having different perceptions and then amplifying those perceptions throughout the organisation by means of political activity. Multiple perceptions thrive when cultures are not strongly shared. Amplifying political activity is destabilising and inevitably bound up with personal career concerns. It becomes difficult to distinguish between functional politics and dysfunctional politics – in practice you cannot separate the two – therefore activity around the strategic issue agenda is highly political. Initially, any potential new line of development involves conflict, as well as a lack of widespread consensus and commitment. In a thriving company there are always potential new lines of development, so there is always conflict and a lack of consensus and commitment around some issue. These are the norms for creative strategic management.

And the important point is that the instability of multiple cultures and conflict around issues and careers, as well as lack of cohesion, consensus and commitment, is vital to the continual provocation of new perceptions. Strategic issues are born out of new perceptions. But in a successful organisation this instability is bounded, not explosive. The boundaries are provided by clear hierarchies, unequally distributed power, different cultures, and the existing business philosophy. Creative strategic management involves continually testing these boundaries. Innovation flows from the creative tension of having boundaries but always testing them.

So, success arises essentially out of a creative tension between the visible stability required to pursue the existing business efficiently on the one hand, and on the other, the far less visible bounded instability, or chaos, required to provoke dynamic strategic issue agenda formation and progression. The tension is that between the simultaneous practice of negative, damping forms of control in short-term closed and contained change situations on the one hand, and the practice of amplifying forms of control in open-ended change situations on the other. An organisation that secures stability in all change situations will not develop active strategic issue agendas. Consequently new strategic directions will not emerge and the organisation will eventually succumb to more imaginative, less orderly rivals. This means that managers have to be able to operate in formal modes according to stable plans at one moment and then switch to informal, unstable political learning activities at the next.

Instability in its bounded form, applied in strategic situations, is of vital importance to the emergence of creative new directions for a company. And this is one of the key discoveries that scientists have made about the operation of creative feedback systems in nature as well.

The importance and nature of spontaneity and self-organisation

The second important feature of the operation of the feedback control loop in open-ended change situations is this: it is impossible to predetermine from the centre what open-ended changes are to be detected and selected for organisational attention. This is because such changes tend to be small and they escalate in ways that depend upon the detail of what the organisation and its rivals do. No central authority can predetermine or direct the course of the political activity, the formation of special interest groups and coalitions, which is necessary for the amplification of some detected change through the organisation. The successful organisation relies on the spontaneous self-organisation of individual managers to detect and select strategic issues for organisational attention. The organisation's strategic issue agenda is built through spontaneous self-organisation.

We can see that this is what actually happens if we consider what managers do at their formal board and top executive meetings. Those institutionalised communication arenas perform a number of functions:

- they review past results against budgets and annual plans, so seeking to explain past success and failure;

- they legitimate proposals for action and resource allocation;

- they perform symbolic functions of approving plans and targets for the existing business as well as proposals to explore potential new activities;

- they attend to administrative matters.

All these functions follow from the central purpose of the board and top executive meetings, namely to oversee and legitimate the operation of the hierarchical control systems and procedures. Indeed, the more efficient the company, the more effective its rules and procedures in delegating authority in predetermined circumstances, the more time the top teams will find that they spend on these functions.

Typically, these functions take up the bulk of the time available at those meetings, thus crowding out what most top executives see as their prime role: that of dealing with the important strategic issues. For this reason we find that formal top team meetings spend 80 to 90 per cent of their time on functions that have very little to do with strategic issues. This outcome is quite predictable. The context of formal meetings in a company practising effective day-to-day control of the business determines that managers at these meetings will spend very little time on the strategic. The group dynamic, one of conformity and dependence, provoked by the formal exercise of authority is not conducive to free-ranging discussion of strategic issues. Such issues will be shelved.

97

What we then find is that strategic issues are dealt with at informal meetings which occur either spontaneously or are at least conducted in very informal ways. The group dynamic on these occasions is very different. Power in its form of authority is not all that much in evidence. Instead we find people using power as influence. The dynamic this provokes is one of more open discussion and learning. This context in terms of group dynamic makes it more likely that strategic issues will be dealt with. It also means that the outcome will not be predictable because small changes in behavioural dynamics can escalate to have important consequences. The role of the institutionalised communication arenas of the business is that of legitimating what emerges from these more informal meetings.

This is not anarchy or explosive instability. It is bounded instability because there are boundaries. These boundaries are provided by:

- the need to gain support and not be out on a limb;
- the existence of hierarchy and power structure;
- different cultures;
- the dynamics of group behaviour.

Self-organisation is not the same thing as formalised widespread participation or power redistribution. It means that key groups of managers find spontaneously that it is worthwhile getting involved in areas outside their formal responsibility because they can themselves see some relevance. And the less this kind of spontaneous activity around open-ended issues is confined to the top level, the more likely the organisation is to develop innovative, new strategic directions.

Building and dealing with the strategic issue agenda is a spontaneous self-organising process that occurs in conditions of bounded instability. It is a political and learning process. It is thinking about, reflecting on and discussing strategic issues informally in groups of managers. It is a process with unpredictable outcomes, because creativity and unpredictability are closely bound together.

HOW CHAOS WILL LEAD MANAGERS TO THINK AND ACT IN A DIFFERENT WAY

The discovery that order can produce chaos and chaos can lead to new order leads us to think and act in a different way in relation to the problem of controlling and developing a business. It does this because it challenges directly the basic, unquestioned assumptions we currently make when we set out to deal with that problem. In Chapter 2 an example was given of what is today's most common approach to that problem. The company concerned was designing its actions to differentiate its business from the competition and control its growth path into the future using a framework of visions and plans.

Changing the basic assumptions

Those frameworks are based on assumptions of the following kind, each of which is contradicted by the properties of nonlinear dynamic systems:

- Long-term futures are knowable. That is, it is possible to know something specific enough about the long-term future of the business to formulate a meaningful vision and set reasonably specific objectives to be achieved at some future point in time. We can gather information and do research that will allow us to make reasonably useful forecasts of what will happen. But when the dynamic is chaotic, then the long-term future is inherently unknowable. It could take just about any form.

- Clear cause and effect relationships exist. That is, business systems, and the market systems they operate in, are driven by laws in which a given cause always produces a given effect. But when the dynamic is chaotic, then it will often be impossible to ascribe an effect we observe to some clear set of causes. The effect may well be the result of many small, chance disturbances which have escalated. Looking back it will be almost impossible to say what caused what.

- The environment is a given reality outside the business and independent of it. This makes it possible to identify that environment, and the changes in it, quite separately from what any individual business does. But when the dynamic is chaotic, the business itself will partly be creating its own environment through creative interactions with other organisations and people in that environment. We would have to know, in advance, the detail of what each business and its competitors, suppliers and customers would do before we could say what some future environment would look like.

- The successful business adapts to its environment. But when the dynamic is chaotic, the business partly creates its environment. It is then not meaningful to talk about adapting to it, for the environment is also adapting to the business.

- Disturbances to stable business performance come mainly from unforeseeable changes in the environment. Because of this, or because managers are incompetent, the performance of a business will be irregular. But when the dynamic is chaotic, irregular performance is a fundamental property of the system.

- It is possible to install structures, systems, rules and procedures which will ensure that mangers identify the long-term consequences of what they are doing and take appropriate action. But when the dynamic is chaotic, each new strategic issue and the responses to it have unknowable consequences requiring a different approach each time. This makes it impossible to install systems and procedures to deal with them.

- Managers at the top of the organisation are in control of the long-term path of the business. But when the dynamic is chaotic, the long term future is unknowable and systems cannot be installed to deal with it. It follows that those at the top cannot control the long term outcomes of change.

- Success comes from maintaining a dynamic, adaptive equilibrium with the environment and the equilibrium of harmony and cohesion within the organisation itself. Success is consistency and cohesive teams. Success is a stable state of order and regularity. But when we think about an organisation in feedback terms, we see that success requires a state of bounded instability, far-from-equilibrium. The dynamic of success is chaotic in the scientific meaning of that term.

When we change so many basic assumptions in so fundamental a way, we will inevitably design our actions in a very different manner. On the old assumptions we design our actions by starting with some future state, either some forecast or some desired state. We identify the gap between where we are now, or would be without changing what we do, and then work back to see what we need to do in order to get to this forecast or desired state. We try to set out what we are going to do in advance of the changes happening. We learn in advance of acting and we embody that learning in plans or visions. We gather information, we do research, we analyse options. We set up rules and procedures ahead of time. We think in terms of detail, using step by step analytical rules. We focus explicit attention on order, harmony, consistency, overall frameworks and blue prints to sustain that order as we move through time. We look for expert opinions. We call for more information. We seek to adapt. And when we succeed in doing all this we simply repeat what we have done before and so in the end we fail.

Learning instead of planning or envisioning

In fact, the successful do something else, usually without fully understanding what they are doing. They act in a manner which is more consistent with the chaos assumptions. If we explicitly adopt the chaos assumptions then we would explicitly design actions in the following ways:

- We would start from the here and now, with challenging aspirations and ambitions, determination and initiative.

- We would go forward from where we are, without trying to work out in advance what will happen.

- We would use intuition, reasoning by analogy, reflection upon experience, to design innovative and creative actions to deal with issues we have detected now; issues we know will have important long-term consequences even if we cannot say what those consequences will be.

- We would act and see how that turns out, dealing with the consequences as they occur. In short we would learn in real time.

- We will become very concerned with:
    how we are learning as teams of managers;
    the nature of the political interaction and the effects that this is having on the group dynamic;
    the impact of personality on learning and deciding.

- We will be concerned, not with adapting to a given world out there, but with making that world different from the way it would have been. Proaction and reaction will lose their meaning, to be replaced by continually creative interaction.

- We will be concerned with creating conditions within which people can learn and act spontaneously, using their own initiative.

When we recognise that the future is unknowable and abandon any attempt to design our actions on spurious forecasts of that future, we do not abandon all concern with the long term. Just because we cannot predict it does not mean that we give up and no longer concern ourselves with it. Instead we realise that we have to create the long term, that we have to learn about it continually and discover it. By focusing the concern on here and now issues that have long-term consequences we actually deal with the long term in a more realistic and creative way. The concern is with what we need to do now, not what we might do at some point in the unknowable future. We become concerned with how to develop challenge and aspiration, spontaneity and difference. And we see that all of this is inconsistent with an exclusive concern with order, stability, harmony and consistency.

We act differently when we cannot plan for the long term while we are playing the game. We discover what to do, we learn, as we go along. Small changes escalate, they may get into vicious and virtuous circles. And because it is unpredictable the game is exciting to play and exciting to watch. The next chapter explores what all this means for the nature of strategic thinking and learning.

REFERENCES

1. Nonaka, I (1988) 'Creating Organizational Order out of Chaos: Self Renewal in Japanese firms', California Management Review, Spring.

2. Pettigrew, A M (1973) *The Politics of Organizational Decision Making*, Tavistock Publications, London.
   Pfeffer, J (1981) *Power in Organizations*, Bakkinger, Cambridge, Ma.
   Kanter, R Moss (1985) *The Change Masters: Innovation in the American Corporation*, Simon & Schuster, Englewood Cliffs, NJ.

3. Thomas, D (1990) *Alan Sugar, The Amstrad Story*, Century, London, p251.

5

Strategic Thinking and Contention

The idea that order can produce chaos and chaos can produce order in creative dynamic systems is a powerful new scientific insight. It has important implications for the nature of strategic thinking in a business. The models of the strategy process, to which most managers today explicitly subscribe, lead to a particular view on what strategic thinking is all about. The dynamic systems perspective provides powerful reasons for rejecting that view and adopting a more useful one.

The new perspective makes it impossible for us to avoid confronting the open-ended nature of the future facing any nonlinear feedback system. The future of such systems is inherently unpredictable. This is because their sensitivity to small changes and their amplifying natures effectively break the links between cause and effect. Humans operating in a system facing unpredictable open-ended futures find it impossible to sustain consensus amongst themselves for other than short time periods around individual issues, unless they substantially suspend their critical faculties. Their prime difficulty is in framing and sharing perceptions of problems and opportunities, not in solving problems. They are confronted not by easily understandable regularity but by irregular patterns similar to those experienced before, but also different.

Effective strategic thinking in these circumstances must, therefore, be based on assumptions of unpredictability, weak cause and effect links, irregular patterns, ill-structured problems and opportunities and continuing contention. The task is one of developing new mental models for each new situation. In contrast, received wisdom focuses on problem-solving, predictability, close cause and effect links, regular patterns, continuing harmony and consensus. The task is seen as one of applying the same general models, techniques and prescriptions to many different situations.

As soon as a successful business is understood to be a dynamic system of the nonlinear feedback type, operating in the chaos border area, strategic thinking has to be seen as:

- continually developing new mental models for each new situation rather than applying the same general prescriptions to many situations;

- reasoning by analogy and intuition around qualitative, irregular patterns rather than analysis and quantification;

- understanding the whole, interconnected system rather than its separate parts;

- anchored to the here and now, not the future;

- focusing on process rather than outcome, on the mental models governing the process itself.

Each of these significant changes in what strategic thinking means will be discussed in turn.

THINKING AND LEARNING – THE USE OF MENTAL MODELS

The ability of humans to assess a situation, and design a response to it, is limited by the capacity of the short-term working memory of the brain. Tests have shown that we are only capable of retaining and processing up to about seven bits of information at any one time.[1] A bit may be a digit or a letter of the alphabet, or some chunk of digits or letters, for example a word. The long-term memory seems to have an infinite capacity, but it takes seconds to store new material in that memory. Our ability, therefore, consciously to process new information and bring to bear already stored information and techniques is severely limited.

So, we cope with the mass of information that constitutes reality by ignoring most of it. We select only what we regard to be the most important features – we construct simplified mental models of reality because this is the only way we can comprehend it and design actions to deal with it. We build up large numbers of models in our memories from past experience and education, which we then use to simplify any new situations we encounter and design actions to respond to them. The limited capacity of the human brain is overcome by building mental models and those models determine how we see the world the next time around and therefore what we do. Those models constitute a frame of reference within which we think, explain, learn, prescribe and act.

We also use another device to overcome our limited brain capacities. We automate a great many of the models we use by pushing them below the level of awareness. Then we call upon them, without thinking about or examining them, to comprehend some situation we find ourselves in and design a response to that situation. So an expert physician notes certain symptoms and then automatically calls up an appropriate mental model to prescribe a treatment. All experts do the same thing – they recognise key features of a category and then automatically call up an appropriate model to design their responses. They do not have to sift consciously through all the models in their brains to select a response.

While this is an efficient way of overcoming the limitations of the brain, it does have a serious drawback. The drawback is that we do not question the assumptions we are making when we use the model. The more automatic and fast, that is the more skilled, our behaviour, the less we question the mental model driving it. And when times are turbulent this failure to question may well be an omission of great importance. Models that have worked in previous situations may not work in the new ones thrown up by rapid change. Coping with open-ended futures and turbulent change requires continual questioning and changing of submerged mental models. Without it there is the very real possibility of skilled incompetence, that is designing actions in a highly automatic way that produces unintended outcomes.

Another way in which we compensate for our limited brain processing capacity is that of sharing mental models. When we work together in groups, we come to share the same implicit models. We tend to make the same unquestioned assumptions as each other when we confront a new situation together. This cuts down on the need to exchange information before we act together. But the drawback is that we mutually reinforce each others' implicit assumptions rather than questioning them. The more skilled a group is in acting together, that is the faster and more automatically it acts, the less people in that group question the assumptions upon which their actions are based. And in turbulent times this could lead to the continuing use of inappropriate models and the designing of ineffective actions. Coping with open-ended futures and turbulent change requires continual questioning and changing of shared mental models. Without this, groups of managers may well display a high degree of skilled incompetence.

Consider how we use these models to cope with chaos.

How we change, develop and use mental models to cope with chaos

A common response to the claim that the dynamic of successful companies is chaotic, is to reject the whole idea. The basis for this rejection is that chaos can have no relevance to human systems because human beings are simply not able to cope with it. This response focuses on the inherent unpredictability of the specific shapes and events that unfold when behaviour is chaotic. What view of human memorising, thinking, deciding and designing actions would lead to this response?

It would be a view in which humans recognise events and shapes according to rigidly defined features. On this view, we put individual items into a particular category if, and only if, the item has all the defining features of the category. A category is then seen as clear cut, containing individuals that are the same in all important respects. We retain those clear category features in our memories and when confronted with another situation we recall those features and so know how to categorise some new phenomenon. As computers do, we store individual items, or at least clear-cut category features, in our memories for use in later situations. In those later situations we recall what has been stored for comparison with what we now observe and we apply step-by-step rules to the individual items observed, to determine how to act in relation to them. The process of learning, then, involves memorising clear-cut bodies of knowledge and formulating explicit step-by-step rules relating causes to effects, that can be applied to new situations. If this is indeed how we perceive, memorise, learn and design actions then we would have severe difficulties in dealing with the unpredictability of specific items that are related to each other only in terms of a fuzzy kind of family resemblance.

But there is evidence that this is not the only, nor even the most important, mode we are mentally capable of operating in. Numerous tests have indicated that our memories do not store information in units representing the precise characteristics of the individual shapes or events we perceive. We store information about the strength of connection between individual units perceived. We chunk information together into categories or concepts using family resemblance type features. We relate new information to old using typical or prototype individual events as a guide to categorisation. We store in terms of relatedness or associative strength. Memory emphasises the general structural content rather than specific content. We categorise information by looking for overlapping features; features that individuals have in common. It has also been noted that we retain memories for exceptions. We remember in terms of deviations from the existing mental models we have stored in our memories. We memorise the irregularities in the patterns we observe. We use previously stored schemas, frames or scenes to fill in the details of what we subsequently observe. We notice analogies between one situation and another, even when the specifics are quite different. We use thematic organisation points, representing high level analogies between situations which are different in detail, but related in structure.[2]

We are capable of generalising spontaneously and we are stimulated to new perspectives by paradoxes, anomalies, contradictions and conflicts. When we confront new situations we build new mental models using analogies with previous ones. The use of analogy in perceiving, classifying and developing new mental models appears to be of great importance in human thinking:

> Analogy pervades thought. ... To make the novel seem familiar by relating it to prior knowledge, to make the familiar seem strange by viewing it from a new perspective – these are fundamental aspects of human intelligence that depend on the ability to reason by analogy. This ability is used to construct new scientific models, to design experiments, to solve new problems in terms of old ones, to make predictions, to control experiments, to construct arguments, and to interpret literary metaphors.[3]

We do not design actions in totally new situations using step-by-step rules in which causes are clearly related to effects – indeed it can be demonstrated that step-by-step rules do not work when it comes to discovering at least certain kinds of new truths.[4] In new situations, we use intuition. We use analogies drawn from past experience upon which we reflect and which we then adapt to suit the new situation. Differences, exceptions and deviations from the expected, play an important part in how we remember and classify the new. The most important form of learning is not that which involves storing detail or step-by-step rules. Complex learning is about developing new mental models, about changing the basic assumptions upon which old mental models are built.

Why chaos is not a problem

Now if we think about humans designing their actions in this manner, then chaotic behaviour presents no real problem. In fact we might even say that the human mind is ideally suited to handling chaotic situations. Since in chaotic systems the individual events are always different, there is no point in storing detailed information on those individual events. What we store instead and subsequently use to design our actions is the vague family resemblances which accompany all the individual differences. We use learning processes of reasoning by analogy, of intuition, of reflecting on experience and adapting it to new situations, all of which are ideally suited to handling chaos.

> Evolution has come up with two broad strategies for solving the problem of allowing complex behaviour. One is to pre-program the organism so that everything that is necessary for efficient functioning is built into the genes of the organism, with a minimum modification if necessary. This occurs in the case of many insects and so-called 'lower organisms'. While such a solution is very rigid, organisms adopting it have been successful for far longer than man has been on the planet, and may well outlive him by a similar margin. The other strategy is to produce an organism which can learn, that is one that can modify behaviour to suit the demands of the environment. The human race is clearly the organism that is most dependent on learning and most flexible in its programming.[5]

What managers need to decide is whether they operate in an environment in which they can survive by adopting the 'insect strategy' of pre-programming, or one that requires the more flexible strategy of 'real-time learning'. If the dynamics of business success are indeed chaotic, then there can be little doubt that it is the real-time learning strategy which is required. And that means a flexible process in which managers deploy intuition, reasoning by analogy and reflection on experience to develop new mental models to deal with new specific situations as they arise. The human mind is well suited to this task. This real-time learning method of designing actions is much more difficult than simply following preprogrammed step-by-step analytical rules. But it is far more effective in chaotic conditions. The obstacles many managers seem to encounter with this real-time learning view of the nature of strategic control may well be the beliefs, currently widespread, that we can only succeed by pre-programming, by reasoning according to step-by-step rules and manipulating large amounts of information stored in detail. We are likely to find the blocks to effective real-time learning in emotional, preconditioning and behavioural factors.

Managers have the mental equipment to cope with chaos and reasoning by analogy rather than analysis holds the key to coping.

Analogy and qualitative patterns versus analysis and quantification

When we confront the uncertain future of a particular business organisation we can approach the problem in one of two different ways:

1. The analytical approach. Conditioned by traditional scientific methodology, we look for cause and effect. For example, we analyse the structure of the industry our particular company is operating in – the barriers to entry of new firms, the availability of substitutes for our product, the power of our suppliers and customers, the intensity of the competition we face. We then identify the particular combinations of these factors that cause successful companies to follow generic strategies of either cost leadership, or product differentiation, or focus on niche markets. Having identified cause and successful effect, we prescribe one of those strategies for our particular business, given the structure of the industry it operates in. There are many techniques available for use in this manner: value chain analysis, product life cycles, product portfolio analysis, learning curves and many more.

The contingency view is another example of direct cause and effect reasoning. Here we conclude that particular environmental features such as rapid growth and high levels of uncertainty require flexible, organic organisational structures to achieve success. On the other hand, mature markets and low levels of uncertainty require more formal, mechanistic structures. Others distinguish different styles of strategic management. Causes in the form of highly uncertain markets, overlapping portfolios of businesses, production processes requiring investments with long-term paybacks require a 'Strategic Management' style, with top-down formal planning, if success is to be achieved. Other causes, such as stable markets, portfolios of separate businesses and short payback investments require a 'Financial Control' style, with tight, short-term budgetary controls, if success is to be achieved.[6]

This approach, then, is that of analytical cause and effect reasoning leading to general predictions and prescriptions that can be applied in many specific instances. It is, of course, recognised that these predictions and prescriptions will only ever be approximate because of the inability to specify the model accurately enough, or to take all relevant factors into account. But the belief is that the models are general and can be applied approximately to many different companies.

When managers come to use these analytical techniques and their predictions, they find it impossible to apply them in this direct cause and effect way. If they try to do so, the result can be unfortunate. In the 1970s, General Foods used product portfolio analysis and reached the conclusion that its coffee business was a commodity cash cow which should not be invested in. This conclusion led it almost to miss the differentiation of the coffee market into specialist types of coffee with high margins.

2.   The analogy approach. Instead of reasoning in direct cause and effect terms, creative managers use the strategic analysis techniques to generate analogies to their own situation. They use categories of strategic behaviour, such as cost leadership or differentiation, to prompt questions and raise issues around the specific action they should now take in a particular company. They look at patterns of development as companies move from small entrepreneurial businesses to more bureaucratic corporations. And they use these typical conclusions to generate perspectives which may guide choices they now have to make in particular circumstances. They are then, I suggest, employing the general qualitative patterns that are part of chaos, to prompt and provoke a range of choices they should now consider in particular circumstances. What is important in the research produced on businesses, is not the analysis, the cause and effect links, but the qualitative descriptions of patterns of behaviour.

When we think of a successful business as one with chaotic dynamics, we stop looking for specific causes and effects leading to general prescriptions. Instead we look for the irregular, but recognisable qualitative patterns in chaos, as prompts to creative choices. Chaos with its specific unpredictability and irregular category patterns, is not a no-hope situation. It is one which we are particularly well equipped to deal with mentally.

Example: differentiation in the electricity industry

An example of how we use this property of recognisable qualitative patterns in business is provided, I believe, by a study of changes occurring in the electricity industry in North America and Europe.[7] The author of that study puts forward the proposition that electricity suppliers will increasingly differentiate their product. There is no definitive model which allows us to predict that such differentiation will occur or what form it will take. So, the author looks for similar circumstances and translates the patterns observed there into ones which might apply to electricity. Those similar circumstances are provided by the airline industry. As with electricity, the product cannot be stored and demand moves from sharp peaks to deep troughs on a daily basis. Airlines have differentiated their products by:

- category of passenger (business and tourist);
- time of use (peak and off peak); and
- level of service (first class and economy).

It is argued that electricity suppliers have been doing much the same thing in terms of customer category and time of use and that they could take this differentiation much further. For example they might introduce low cost, low service products with interruptible supply. This is not a prediction of what will happen but a guide that managers in the electricity industry might consider in forming judgements on the creative changes they are trying to make in their business.

What we are doing here is using experience of similarity and difference in one place to draw conclusions about possible actions in another place. We do much the same thing when we form expectations of the behaviour of a group of people at some time from experience of another at other times –

we know it will not be exactly the same but there will be some similarity. As management consultants move from one assignment to another, they accumulate models of general personality types and general group interactions. When they see a highly authoritarian manager, they expect either submissive or rebellious interactions. They have no idea how these interactions will develop in specific terms, but they are not completely surprised at the outcomes.

The key point is that creative managers develop new mental models to design actions for each new strategic situation they confront. They develop these models from their experience, using qualitative similarities. But that experience has to be continually re-examined, reflected upon and re-interpreted, if it is to be applied to a new situation.

WHOLE, INTERCONNECTED SYSTEMS RATHER THAN SEPARATE PARTS

The model of strategic thinking presented by the planning and visionary approaches is essentially a reductionist one. That is, it prescribes thinking processes in which the problems and opportunities to be dealt with are split down into their constituent parts and handled in a step-by-step fashion. Here we think about each separate part of the business, identifying key success factors, generating action options and selecting appropriate ones for each of those parts. We analyse each market segment, identifying each element of its structure. We reason about the opportunities and threats each presents and select a suitable focus. We then analyse each function of the business, each aspect of our resource capability, identifying strengths and weaknesses and how capability needs to be matched to market requirements. The result of that thinking is then embodied in hierarchies of plans for business units and for their functions, together aggregating into the corporate plan.

Alternatively, in the visionary mode we think in terms of an overarching vision. Then we identify action steps to realise that vision. We think about the consequences of those actions before we proceed to the next ones. Thinking proceeds in a straight line cause and effect mode, relating behaviour to an outcome.

The insight provided by dynamic system complexity is that the behaviour of a system cannot be understood simply by examining its parts. In effect the system has a life of its own. It has a major impact on behaviour and therefore on outcomes. Thinking has to proceed in terms of whole systems, their interconnections, and the patterns of behaviour they may generate. The point about complex dynamic systems is that changes accumulate slowly out of the interconnections between the constituent parts. Focusing on snapshots of the parts, looking for cause and effect links that are close together in time and space, means missing the slow accumulation of change. Instead of trying to understand the quantitative detail of the parts it is far more fruitful to understand the qualitative nature of the interconnections and the patterns of behaviour. The greatest benefit is to understand the points in the system that are most sensitive and amplifying – the points of greatest leverage. By operating at these points rather than trying to control the detail everywhere, the greatest changes in the system may be brought about.

Business systems are usually more complex than any one person can fully comprehend. But it is quite possible for each of a number of people to contribute to something they do not fully understand. Such interaction can produce results which no single individual can foresee. Thinking in systems terms brings three important insights:

1. When things go wrong, this may be due to system complexity – there may be no one who is to blame.
2. An individual can make a big difference because the structure of the system may well amplify an individual contribution out of all proportion.
3. Operating in complex systems that no one individual fully understands makes cooperation vital and renders automatic competition dangerous.

Simulating the patterns of behaviour generated by a complex system can be a useful aid to thinking in systems terms. It is a tool for playing with patterns to develop analogies and insights of a qualitative kind. But simulating cannot be a tool for predicting when the dynamic is chaotic because such systems have too many possible futures.

THE HERE AND NOW VERSUS THE FUTURE

The current received wisdom on strategic thinking is that it is primarily an intellectual exercise in exploring what is likely to happen. It is an exercise in information processing, in analysis and in forecasting future outcomes. If this approach is to be more than an entertaining fantasy then it can only be applied to systems whose behaviour is predictable. And predictability is only a possibility when cause and effect links can be identified and at least approximately measured. It is only then that we can link a present state through events and actions to a future state as the long-term planning model proposes. It is only then that we can link a future state back to a method of acting as the visionary/ideological model prescribes.

As soon as measurable connections of a practical nature between cause and effect, between action and outcome, become impossible to identify, then there is no point in conjecturing about the future. The future is completely unpredictable. It is *truly* unknowable, and it is absolutely impossible to reason back from a desired future state to the actions required to produce it.

Since thinking about the future is a pointless exercise for an innovative company with its chaotic dynamics, strategic thinking has to be based firmly on the qualitative nature of what is happening now and what has happened in the past. Strategic thinking then focuses on anomalies in the current situation. It is about:

- generating new perspectives on what has been and is going on;

- framing problems and opportunities;

- noticing potential and possibility;

For example, noticing that plastic covers for record players are being made inefficiently by one process when a more efficient process is already available or observing the potential for developing an integrated parcel delivery system to replace a fragmented, ineffective one. Strategic thinking is developing creative new ideas in the here and now, not vainly trying to predict the unknowable.

MENTAL MODELS GOVERNING THE LEARNING PROCESS ITSELF

Inevitably strategic choices are made in open-ended situations where opportunities and problems are difficult to identify and frame; where changes are often small with consequences that gradually accumulate into major developments; where links between causes and effects are lost in the detail of what happens. Successful choice depends upon effective strategic thinking and learning. To be effective it has to be a process of continually identifying small changes and exploring their consequences. But even more important is the surfacing, examination and altering of the frame of reference through which managers perceive the significance of those small changes. That frame of reference is a set of basic, unconscious and therefore rarely questioned assumptions on what it is important to look for, how to interpret what is found, and even more basically, how to think and learn in the first place. The way all of us conduct our thinking and learning activities is determined by some mental model or programme we have acquired on how to think and learn.

We need to distinguish between simple single loop learning and complex double loop learning. We perform single loop thinking and learning when we solve identified problems. We develop a solution and then we test the solution. We perform an action and then learn from the outcome of the action. Single loop learning is about solutions and outcomes. When we perform it we retain the same mental model, the same assumptions and techniques, without questioning. We simply develop different solutions and produce different outcomes. This is the learning mode most of us use most frequently. Managers use it when they monitor their actions against a plan, learning about the effects of their actions, and then taking corrective action. Managers use it when they follow a vision. Here they are not questioning the assumptions on which their actions are based or the manner in which they are learning. They focus on outcomes and do something about them as a result of what they have learned from the monitoring process.

When we perform complex or double loop learning, we enquire into and question the mental model, the assumptions. It is about posing questions rather than finding answers or producing outcomes. It is about looking from a different perspective; about framing problems and opportunities in a different way. In doing so we develop new mental models for newly perceived situations. Managers perform this kind of learning when they identify and develop an innovation. For example, Ibuka, one of the founders of Sony, questioned the assumption that radios weighed 10–20 pounds and came up with the pocket sized radio. He questioned the assumption that mini televisions would not sell.

Kobayishi, also of Sony, questioned assumptions about organisational structures and produced a cell structure of vertical and horizontally interconnected teams. Complex learning is about questioning assumptions and changing mindsets and it is this form of learning that is relevant to strategic situations. This way we are able to cope with the chaos required for creativity.

At the deepest level the problems we have with strategic thinking relate to the learning model we unconsciously use. Studies have shown that, when managers confront open-ended situations, they display a very widespread tendency to use a learning model that is appropriate only in closed and contained change situations.[8] That model is referred to as single loop learning because the learning feedback runs from actions to their outcomes and consequences and back to some responding action again. The second loop is rarely activated. That second loop is one of reflecting upon the implications of action outcomes for the manner in which we are interpreting those outcomes, for the frame of reference we are using. Where we are learning in conditions of predictability, where cause and effect links are reasonably clear, then single loop learning suffices; it is enough to learn simply about outcomes. But when the consequences are unknowable and cause and effect links extremely unclear, it becomes vital to enquire into the very manner in which we are perceiving what is going on.

When a manager designs his or her actions using a single loop learning model, he or she does so in the following manner. He or she approaches the choice situation, which always involves others as well, on the assumption that:

- he or she is there to win and not lose;
- he or she should secure unilateral control of the choice situation;
- and he or she should suppress any emotion or negative feelings about colleagues and their motives.

The last assumption is made on the basis that people should make choices in a rational manner untainted with emotion and that expression of negative feelings will make others defensive, so turning them into opponents.

Because everyone at the choice situation approaches the task with this same set of assumptions, they all tend to adopt tactics of persuasion and selling, listening only superficially to others. They also use face-saving devices for themselves and each other and avoid testing publicly the assumptions they are making about each others' motives or statements. This behaviour produces what has been called skilled incompetence – skilled in that the behaviour is automatic; incompetent in that it produces obstacles to real learning in open-ended situations. These obstacles are all manner of organisational defence routines that become embedded in behaviour and are extremely difficult to change.

Defence routines

The prime defence routine is to make matters undiscussable and to make the fact that they are undiscussable itself undiscussable. So, subordinates refrain from telling their superiors the truth if those superiors are thought likely to react badly. And subordinates do not publicly admit that they are doing this. Ask a group of managers whether they tell their bosses the truth and the usual response is raucous laughter at your *naïveté* – this particular defence routine is widespread indeed. And of course superiors know that this is going on because they do it themselves. The result is an undiscussed game of pretence in which all indulge and all know they are doing it. This routine does, however, provide work for consultants. Because superiors know that their subordinates will not tell them the truth they hire consultants to interview and hold workshops with their subordinates. The bosses know that their subordinates are more likely to open up to outsiders.

Defence routines take the form of bypasses, cover-ups and games. For example, a manager may ask a colleague with whom he or she disagrees for comprehensive proof of a proposal outcome when it is quite clear to all that such proof is impossible to provide. On one occasion I took part in a game that went on for nearly a year. One faction thought that the company should diversify the range of its activities. Another faction led by the chairman thought that it should not. However the chairman did not openly quash the idea. He called for a paper setting out general diversification principles. After discussion at the formal executive meeting, specific proposals were called for – the principles paper was held to be too general. When the specific proposals were discussed, the chairman called for a discussion of the general principles. So it went on and needless to say, no diversification occurred. All of us involved knew it was a game and while we admitted this to each other in groups of twos or threes, no one ever raised it at the full meetings.

Long-term plans, mission statements and visions are games of a similar kind. They are usually abstract statements without operational content, simply to convey an impression of rational decision making and to keep people quiet or feeling more secure.

Perhaps the most popular cover-up, mostly unconscious, is to espouse a different model of learning while actually using the one just described. So, a manager says that he or she is looking for team decision making, that he or she is open to different views and then becomes visibly annoyed when such views are put forward. That manager makes it clear by behaving in a particular manner that team decision making is not actually to occur despite any statements made to the contrary.

This kind of behaviour becomes so entrenched in organisations that it comes to be viewed as an inevitable part of human nature. Managers make self-fulfilling prophecies about what will happen at meetings concerned with open-ended issues – because they claim it is human nature, they indulge in the game playing, so confirming their belief in human nature. The defence routines, game playing and cover-ups can become so disruptive that managers actually avoid discussing contentious open-ended issues altogether. Even if this extreme is not reached, the dysfunctional learning behaviour blocks the detection of gradually accumulating small changes, the surfacing of different perspectives, the thorough testing of proposals through dialogue. Using this learning model, managers struggling to deal with strategic issues end up preparing long lists of strengths and weaknesses, opportunities and threats that simply get them nowhere. They produce mission statements that are so bland as to be meaningless, visions not connected to reality and long-term plans that are simply filed. Or they may decide on an action and then not implement it.

Managers collude in this behaviour and refrain from discussing it. They then distance themselves from what is going on and blame others or the system when things go wrong. They look for solutions in general models, techniques, vision and plans. All the while the real causes of poor strategic management – the learning process itself, the political interaction and the group dynamic – remain stubbornly undiscussable.

And when managers do try to grapple with what is going on, the most common response is to swing to the complete opposite of the single loop learning model described above. Managers try to work on the assumption that everyone should be involved in everything, that all should win, that feelings and emotions should be freely expressed. Behaving on these assumptions simply immobilises decision making and learning.

Surfacing and explaining learning behaviours

The key to effective strategic management is the second learning loop. This involves surfacing and exploring the learning behaviours and organisational defences just discussed and trying to identify the mental models leading to the way problems and opportunities are being framed. The second loop is developing a different learning model and changing mindsets. The behaviour here is one of openness, real listening and a willingness to change one's mind. Individuals strongly advocate their positions, but at the same time invite others to test those positions. Attributions about the motives of others are exposed together with the evidence for that attribution. This is not a free-for-all display of feelings and emotions, but a disciplined attempt to test the undiscussable matters that could be blocking the learning process.

As soon as we recognise that a successful business is a nonlinear feedback system operating in chaos, we have to accept that the future is unknowable and that cause and effect links are very obscure. Consequently we cannot apply general models to each new specific strategic situation. We have to develop a new mental model for each new situation. That is, we have continually to learn in the sense of exposing the assumptions we are making and testing them through open dialogue with others. This whole process is impossible if we employ single loop learning, dealing simply with outcomes and not exploring how we are learning, the assumptions we are making, the defences we are erecting, the games we are playing. These make it impossible to detect small changes, because we make the truth undebatable. They make it impossible to develop new mental models. Since the future is unknowable we have to keep discovering afresh what to do. If we do not continually overcome learning obstacles, we cannot discover what to do. The key to strategic management is enabling groups to learn and discover. This is a continuing process because open-ended change provokes anxiety and immediately invokes single loop learning. It is not conflict that is the problem, it is covering it up that causes the difficulties.

THE IMPACT OF GROUP BEHAVIOUR ON LEARNING

In open-ended situations, learning has to be a group process, not an individual expert or visionary one. In complex, ambiguous situations no one individual is likely to possess wide enough perspectives, as such perspectives are developed through group interaction. Part of the effective learning process, therefore, involves continual examination of how we are interacting.

It is not analytical thinking ability that will determine whether managers attend to open-ended issues, what issues they will attend to or what conclusion they will reach. All these things depend far more fundamentally on how managers are interacting with each other in the groups they form. Yet, while managers show great concern about information flows and analysis, they tend to pay very little attention to how they are interacting. They spend very little time trying to explore the assumptions they are making when they learn together. In all my strategy consultancy assignments, the real problems have had very little to do with information or analysis or individual intellectual abilities. They have always arisen from the interaction and hence learning problems managers experience. And yet these matters are rarely seen as essentially part of the process of strategic management itself. They are parcelled off as organisation behaviour or change management as if these were separate areas of concern. The strategic management process is fundamentally a complex learning process, and it is basically a self-organising one in conditions far-from-equilibrium.

The group learning experience depends on who participates by making comments, asking questions, donating interpretations. Learning depends on the content of such contributions. It also depends upon the context and sequence in which they occur. Usually there will not be one individual consciously and successfully guiding the process to a predetermined end. What each individual learns in such situations depends only partly on his or her own reflections and thinking processes – it depends significantly on how he or she and the other members of the group are interacting with each other. It depends upon the combination of personalities in the group and the behavioural dynamics of the group, on the emotions contributing to and provoking those dynamics, on triggers to the unconscious mind. High levels of uncertainty, lack of structure and insecurity are all known to lead to bizarre group behaviours which can prevent that group from functioning as a working learning group.[9] The learning that occurs within a group will also depend significantly on the culture which that group has developed – the basic assumptions which the members of that group share on how to proceed, on how things are to be done, on what is important and what is not.[10] This shared culture is the retained memory of the group and it has a powerful effect on how it proceeds.

Example: the electricity industry

An example of this learning process is provided by a group of top managers in one of the UK's electricity companies that was about to be privatised. Those managers were exploring ways of improving the margins they could earn on their electricity product. Since it is a commodity they were discussing possibilities for differentiating it.

The situation they found themselves in was open-ended in just about every respect. The kind of electricity market they were having to operate in had never existed before and did not exist anywhere else in the world. The chief executive started the discussion by drawing attention to a study that drew parallels between differentiation of airline products and possible differentiation in electricity. Two other colleagues then joined in and started talking about the technology that would be necessary to differentiate electricity by time of use. The discussion proceeded for some time before one of the quietest members of the group suggested that the whole basis of the comparison between airlines and electricity was invalid. That interjection opened up the way for colleagues who had not yet expressed their views. Then one of their more vociferous colleagues suggested that differentiation could best be secured by adding customer features such as installation of appliances, and he attached this issue to the need for coordinated marketing. This was seen by the others as a bid for increased power and the discussion switched to organisational matters.

Later meetings then resumed the discussion on the very ambiguous and ill-structured issue of differentiation. Gradually concrete proposals for product differentiation emerged.

These managers were learning, in a group context, about a very complex strategic issue. The somewhat random process of discussion was serving the valuable function of bringing different perspectives to bear on the issue. Eventually, out of this process there might come concrete proposals attracting support – or the idea might be abandoned after wide-ranging discussion. In my experience this example is typical of the early stages of handling strategic issues. Out of initial wide-ranging and random discussion, there emerges more precise requirements for information and proposals for action. And that initial random stage can go on for a long time – there is nothing predetermined about it. It depends upon spontaneous self-organisation.

It is possible to instruct a group of people to learn some simple rote task, technique or body of data and ensure that they do it by testing them and then rewarding or punishing them. It is not possible to compel any group of people to learn anything more complex than this. To succeed and innovate an organisation requires groups of people who perform complex learning through which they discover and choose new perspectives, new ideas, new ways of doing things. This process has to be spontaneous and whether or not it occurs depends on the context within which the group is working. Such complex learning processes also cannot be organised in some step by step, orderly fashion. This is because in complex situations no one can know what the group is trying to learn, to discover. The learning process starts without a clear specific purpose of what is to be learned or even how it is to be learned. What purposes the group develops, what it learns and how it learns all depend on the context in which its members are working. The process is spontaneous and self-organising and part of what the group learns is its purpose and the method through which it should be learning.

Instability and learning

Interactive thinking, learning and choosing in a group context is governed by feedback loops which have amplifying and damping properties. A comment made by one member can irritate another who responds, perhaps by attack on some other front or by withdrawal from the discussion. In this way consequences are amplified and what is learned, what the outcome of the group interaction turns out to be, is therefore frequently a matter of chance. The properties of chaos apply to learning in a group context. Complex learning only occurs when the nature of the feedback loops governing the learning is such that they are far-from-equilibrium. People spark new ideas off each other when they argue and disagree, when they are conflicting, confused and searching for a new meaning.

Far-from-equilibrium instability is a precondition for the kind of learning that provokes new meanings. And in these circumstances people display categories of behaviour that we all recognise. One category of behaviour might be avoiding the issues and another might be conflict around the issues. These categories are recognisable, but the specific course they take is unpredictable. People do not provoke new insights when their discussions are characterised by orderly equilibrium states of conformity and dependence on the one hand, or completely disorderly states of rivalry and avoidance on the other.

Because the learning system of a successful group is far-from-equilibrium, it is highly sensitive to the context within which it occurs. And amongst the most important elements of the context are the personality composition and behavioural dynamic of the group, as well as the shared assumptions people make when they interact and learn in a group.

Personality type

Some personality types are comfortable with open-ended issues. Other personality types look for high degrees of analytical security before they are willing to progress an issue. Some personality types prefer to keep options open, while others always look for immediate closure. Some personality types think intuitively and others rely heavily on formal logic. Some rely on feelings while others always want the facts.

Consequently the learning styles of individuals differ markedly. The kinds of issues a given group will deal with, what they will try to avoid, the manner in which they deal with issues they do attend to, how successful they are, will then depend significantly on the composition of the group

123

in personality terms. Small changes in personality composition, the removal of one person or the addition of another, can have a major impact on the outcome of their work together. One person behaving in a neurotic manner can completely disrupt the work of the group. Because of this sensitivity to who is there and how they behave, the outcomes of group work, when open-ended change is being dealt with, depend on chance and are unpredictable in specific terms.

But there are recognisable patterns in individual behaviours. We can recognise the personality category types, even though we cannot predict specific behaviour. And the same point applies to categories of interaction between people.

Categories of group dynamic

Some typical patterns of group dynamic have been identified by researchers. One well known study explains the behaviour of a group in terms of two levels.[11] At one level, the conscious apparent level, the group is focusing on the work in hand, the tasks it has come together to perform. But at the unconscious level, the behaviour of individuals in the group is affected by a basic assumption, an atmosphere which affects how they work together. They may be unconsciously affected by the fight–flight assumption. Here the underlying dynamic is one of either intense conflict or the complete avoidance of conflict. Or the assumption may be one of dependence, where the group is looking for leadership. Or it may be one of pairing in which most of the group is observing an interchange between two of their number, hoping that this will yield the answer they are looking for. And different basic assumptions are appropriate to different tasks. Where the group is concerned with closed change, a basic assumption of dependence and the compliance that accompanies this will make it more effective. Where the group is concerned with open-ended issues a basic assumption that results in some conflict is more likely to be helpful. When structures are removed and the group faces considerable uncertainty, the basic assumptions can come to dominate behaviour in the group so that it is incapable of any work at all. And a group can switch in a volatile manner from one basic assumption to another.

It is open-ended change situations that are most likely to provoke group dynamics which are obstructive to dealing with the issues.

What happens to an open-ended issue will depend on highly complex interpersonal relationships in groups. Groups to which one might apply, at a particular time, the labels of 'fight–flight' will obviously not deal with open-ended issues at that time. Groups showing a high level of dependence may not develop wide enough perspectives to handle such issues effectively.

It is not unusual for managers to abandon meetings trying to deal with open-ended issues because they simply do not function. One of my clients, in the electronics industry, called an informal meeting of top executives to discuss reorganisation proposals. That group accomplished nothing in two days of meetings because they did little but fight over the proposals. That chief executive thereafter avoided such informal meetings. On another occasion, the first two strategy workshops I facilitated with a top management team involved little but the others listening to a discussion between the chief executive and myself. It was only when we brought in other people that the dynamic changed. On another occasion in the same industry faced with massive changes, the top team did little but avoid any serious issues for three meetings. The underlying conflict between them made it too dangerous to talk about any of the issues in a serious way.

Such dynamics show the essential properties of chaos. There are recognisable categories of group dynamic, but the specific behaviours over time are unpredictable. What happens during meetings will, therefore, often be very difficult to explain. A well timed remark, or even a purely chance remark, could divert the whole course of the discussion and the approach to the issue into completely different and unexpected directions. Small interventions could escalate and have a major impact on the eventual outcome.

HOW CHAOS WILL LEAD MANAGERS TO THINK AND ACT IN A DIFFERENT WAY

Understanding a business in terms of dynamic feedback systems provides a very different perspective on the nature of strategic thinking and learning to that which currently dominates the views of managers. It is a perspective that focuses attention on the group learning process itself, the assumptions driving that process and the deeply embedded organisational obstacles to that process. How groups of managers interact and learn together becomes the key to effective strategic management. The dynamic systems perspective results in a major shift in emphasis:

- away from a concern with the individual expert or visionary to a concern with the effect of personality, group dynamics and learning behaviours of managers in groups;

- from the stability of continuing consensus based on 'rational' reasoning to the creative instability of contention and dialogue with the periodic consensus it produces around particular issues;

- away from condemning the messiness of real life business decision making as dysfunctional politics and then ignoring it, to examining, understanding and dealing with organisational defence mechanisms and game playing;

- away from a perception of organisational learning as a simple process relating to outcomes to an understanding of organisational learning as a complex process of continually questioning how we are learning;

- away from the closure of problem solving to the opening up of contentious and ambiguous issues;

- away from trying to apply general prescriptive models to many specific situations, to developing new mental models to design actions for each new strategic situation.

REFERENCES

1. Baddeley, A (1990) *Human Memory, Theory and Practice*, Lawrence Earlbaum Associates.

2. Baddely, op. cit.

3. Gick, M L & Holyoak, K J (1983) 'Schema introduction and analogical transfer', Cognitive Psychology, vol 15, pp1–38.

4. Penrose, R (1989) *The Emperor's New Mind*, Oxford University Press, Oxford.

5. Dawkins, R (1988) *The Blind Watchmaker*, Penguin, London, p198.

6. Goold, M & Campbell, A (1988) *Strategies and Styles*, Blackwell, Oxford.

7. Sioshansi, F (1990) 'Pricing and Marketing Electricity', The Economist Intelligence Unit, January.

8. Argyris, C (1990) *Overcoming Organizational Defenses: Facilitating Organizational Learning*, Allen & Bacon, Needham Heights, Ma.

9. Bion, W (1961) *Experiences in Groups and Other Papers*, London Tavistock Publications, London.

10. Schein, A (1985) *Organizational Culture and Leadership*, Jossey-Bass, San Francisco.

11. Bion, W op. cit.

6

Strategic Intention and Unpredictability

Over the past twenty years managers and researchers have been re-interpreting what the successful do when they manage strategically. This has led to new insights and prescriptions on business strategy formation.

PLANS

The interpretation that practising managers most prominently subscribe to, is some form of long-term planning. But there has been a distinct move away from detailed quantitative plans prepared by 'experts', to a much looser view of planning as a flexible, qualitative function of profit responsible line managers. Instead of fixed, quantitative long-term objectives, managers are urged to prepare mission statements. Instead of projecting financial variables and using simple portfolio techniques, managers are encouraged to use more realistic frameworks to analyse industry structures, value chains and sources of competitive advantage and competitive capability. Strategic management has come to be seen as an analytical process to establish sustainable competitive positions. The overall conceptual framework of what the business is all about, what it stands for and what it is trying to achieve in qualitative terms has become more important than formal procedures and quantification.

Perspectives on the role of top management in this more flexible process have widened. That role is seen by some to be an active, directing one concerned with content. It is setting both the long-term objectives and the route to be adopted in achieving them – top down corporate planning. Others see the role in less directing terms as far as the content of strategy is concerned. Here top managers provide an umbrella; they set very general targets and guidelines on content and boundaries, and allow other organisational actors to develop strategies within them. Then there are those who see the role of top management as largely confined to the process of long-term planning rather than the content. Here it is the planning process itself that is controlled from the top through staffing, structure, procedural rules and resource allocation, leaving the content to other organisational actors. Which of these top management roles is most appropriate is said to depend upon how uncertain the environment is.

Visions and ideology

Others take the re-interpretation in a different direction. As an addition to, or a replacement of, long-term planning, strategy formation is presented as the achievement of predetermined, qualitative visions of future states. The mechanisms for achieving the vision are seen as strongly shared ideologies and widespread participation in incremental trial and error action. Such action is to be logically connected to the existing business and fall within the vision and ideology criteria.

Emergent strategy

In more recent years, the re-interpretation of strategy formation has been taken even further. Some have been presenting strategy formation as a direction that emerges from the tactics which a company follows;[1] or as a revolution in what the company does rather than a series of incremental actions;[2] or as the ideas and actions of individual organisational actors that converge on a common theme.[3] The idea underlying these interpretations is one of patterns in action that emerge, or evolve, over the long term. Organisational actors converge on the same theme so that it pervades the organisation without any prior central intention or continuing control. Strategies derive from collective action, from which organisational actors jointly learn, rather than prior, central, shared intention. Writers on emergent strategy stress that this does not mean that control is absent. It means that managers are open, flexible, responsive and willing to learn. In line with the idea of emergent strategy there has recently been an increasing interest in the concept of the learning organisation.

A spectrum of possibilities

So, we have now reached the stage where strategy formation can be seen in terms of a spectrum that stretches from the organisationally intended at one end to the emergent at the other. In stable, predictable environments it will be appropriate to develop strategies in organisationally intended ways. In highly stable conditions, strategies may be planned – or strategies may be developed in an ideological or visionary manner as conditions become rather less stable and predictable. At the other extreme of the spectrum we get strategy emerging from organisational learning processes, when an environment is too unstable or complex to comprehend fully, or too imposing to defy. Learning then enables managers to act before everything is fully understood, so responding to an evolving reality rather than focusing on a stable fantasy. Whereas the organisationally intended strategies flow from central direction and hierarchy or ideology, emergent ones result from convergent behaviour and collective action.[4] The advice is for managers to adapt their approach to strategy formation according to the environmental conditions they face. Sometimes this will mean encouraging learning activities so that strategies can emerge.

These more recent views on strategy formation as a shifting process that includes emergence through group learning, have yet to attract much explicit attention from most practising managers. As soon as one labels strategy formation as emergent, most seem to assume that this means there is nothing further for them to do. What will emerge will emerge, so managers had better concentrate on the intentional aspects, seems to be the view.

The implications of dynamic systems thinking

The purpose of this chapter is to explore what dynamic systems thinking implies for the possibility of forming strategies by employing the organisationally intended modes of planning and envisioning. The dynamic systems perspective provides reasons for concluding that innovative, new strategies cannot be organisationally intended; they can only emerge.

In most of the discussions I have had with senior managers and consultant colleagues during our work together on strategy assignments, there has been considerable confusion caused by each of us having different conceptions of what we mean by 'strategy', 'intention', 'planning the long-term future of a company', 'vision', 'mission', 'values' and many other related words. And the confusion persists unless we expose and clarify what the different conceptions are, what unquestioned assumptions they are based on, and what circumstances those conceptions and assumptions are appropriate to. Careful consideration of what these words mean is of great practical importance – the meaning we attach to these terms has a critical impact on the strategic management actions we design. Consider first then what strategy means.

THE MEANING OF 'STRATEGY'

In a very general sense, the *strategies* of a company are the *perceived patterns*, over a long time period, in the *sequences of actions* undertaken by managers in that company. Strategic actions have widespread, long-term consequences that establish the *shape* of the company and its *position* in relation to its customers, competitors, suppliers and regulators. The company's shape and position determine its *performance*. The strategy is the pattern in actions. The result of the strategy is the shape and position of the company. Together shape and position determine performance. And 'strategy' is essentially a dynamic concept: it is a continually changing pattern over time in company actions, provoking actions on the part of other organisations and individuals in the environment, in turn requiring reactions on the part of the company. Strategy is an endless feedback loop connecting actions, consequences and reactions through time.

Long-term planning is one mode of forming the pattern in action that is strategy. Establishing visions and strong ideologies is another mode. Both are organisationally intended modes where that intention relates to a whole set of key issues. Yet another mode is convergent learning and political interaction through which patterns in action emerge. Here there are individual and organisation sub-unit intentions, but organisational intention itself emerges around particular issues.

Example: Christian Salvesen

This UK cold storage and distribution company started life as a general shipbroking and owning company in 1864. By the end of the last century the major part of the business was focused on marine coal transport. Then in the early part of this century the company developed a whaling business as an extension of its shipping activities. This was to become the largest whaling company in the world. Over the same period, the coal transport business was gradually phased out. The whaling business required floating factories to process whale products. As this century proceeded, the whaling business was phased out because of competition, restrictions on fishing rights and popular disapproval of whaling. As the whaling business began to decline in relative importance, the refrigerated floating factories were developed to process other fish products. By the time this fish processing operation was terminated in 1967, the company had developed into land-based cold storage and distribution activities. In 1960 Christian Salvesen entered into a small property development activity that was to evolve into a large house building operation.

When we look back on the development of this company, we can describe its strategy as one of concentric diversification away from the original shipbroking business. The pattern in actions was one of developing in a number of different directions from an original core, some in closely related steps and some in less clearly related steps. We can take snapshots of this dynamic pattern at particular points in time and what we then see is a shape to the business and a position in relation to the business's customers, competitors, suppliers and regulators. A snapshot in 1980 reveals a company shape in which the predominant activities are cold storage and distribution, with relatively less important activities in house building. The snapshot also reveals a position in terms of shares in the cold storage, distribution and housing markets. This shape and market position determines the performance of the company.

It is not necessary to take a century to perceive strategy as pattern in actions. If we take any five to ten year period in the development of Christien Salvesen we will detect patterns that we might label as diversification, differentiation, focusing or cost leadership.

The question to be discussed now is, how future shape and position (and hence performance) is determined and how the pattern of actions leading to them is formed. The answer which the great majority of managers give to this question is that the future strategy, or pattern, must be intended. What does this mean?

ORGANISATIONAL INTENTION

In its fullest sense, organisational intention means that:

- at least key groups of managers are deliberately sharing an intention to achieve some relatively distant future state relating to shape, position and performance and

- they are deliberately sharing an intention to achieve that future state through a particular strategy, that is pattern in actions.

Organisationally intending a future state means that managers have:

- established what the future state (shape, position, performance) of the business is to be at the start of some long-term time period, say five years, and held that intention in a relatively constant form throughout the period. Intention is prior and stable over time. If key managers keep changing the intended end state as they proceed through the time period, then they are in effect discovering it as they act. The intention is emergent not predetermined;

- set out the future state in a reasonably specific, unambiguous form so that it is possible to say at a later date whether they achieved it or not;

- related the intended future state to some picture of the environment in which it is to be achieved. The end state must be anchored in some way to reality;

- established a future state that covers the business as a whole. That state must be overarching and central to the business. If we find many different, unconnected aims then managers may be intending many different specific responses to many different changes, but they will not be intending the future state of the organisation as a whole;

- consciously shared the intended future state throughout the time period so that all knew what they were striving for. If instead of a shared overarching future state, we have a number of individual or sub-unit intentions then the future state realised will have emerged from the interaction between those individuals and sub-units. That state will not have resulted from organisational intention;

- deliberately used the intended future state to govern their actions so that connections can be demonstrated between what they did and the state achieved. If this condition is not satisfied, the end state may have emerged from a number of individual intentions, or even chance events;

- set out a unique future state. Managers only intend success. In most markets today, firms survive and succeed when they deliver products which are different in some sense to those of competitors. The intended end state must therefore be a unique one, differentiating the company from its competitors.

If in addition to an intended future state, the strategy itself is to be intended, then the developments leading up to that future state also have to be reasonably predictable. If we cannot foresee the pattern in action and consequences, then we cannot intend it. It will emerge from the detail of what we do and any pattern will be evident only with hindsight.

Organisational intention here has to do with conscious, purposeful, deliberate design of both the future state and the actions leading to that state. It has to do with a concept of predetermined direction covering the business as a whole and shared by key groups of decision makers.

No one, to my knowledge, seriously suggests that any business could be controlled and developed over the long term in a fully intentional manner. Instead, the assumption is that it is possible to get close enough to the conditions for intentionality at least to enable the selection of a reasonably useful future state or vision. And it seems a natural assumption to make when the only alternative is thought to be haphazard action or short-term reaction. But there is another possible alternative – that of emergence. The practically useful juxtaposition is that of intentionality and emergence. It is perfectly possible for future states and patterns of action to emerge from the continuing interactions between people and groups operating in a complex system. And this need not be haphazard.

In his book, 'Managing on the Edge', Richard Pascale[5] describes how Ford transformed itself in the 1980s from a huge loss maker to a profitable and acclaimed excellent company. It is a story of a number of independent initiatives on quality, design, employee participation, executive development, studies on Japanese competitors, management workshops and many more, that somehow came together in a mutually reinforcing way. All of this happened in conditions of conflict and tension and there was no central plan or vision. The outcome emerged from many individual intentions and actions. Pascale describes what happened as the coincident unfolding of events where it is impossible to envision that coincidence without the benefit of hindsight. The idea of some form of intention and patterns in action emerging from the detail of actions and interactions is therefore not at all far-fetched.

There is, then, a spectrum of possibilities. At one end of the spectrum all the conditions for full intentionality are satisfied – managers can then establish in advance what the long-term outcome will be and they can identify in advance the pattern of actions necessary to get them there. The mode of strategic management is that of long-term planning. At the other end of the spectrum none of the conditions are satisfied – managers then have no idea of what the long-term outcome will be and they can only detect the pattern in what they have done with the benefit of hindsight. In this case the strategy will emerge from the detail of what they do. The mode for emergent strategy is a process of discovery: of learning from what is done; of deciding what to do through a process of real time learning and political interaction. Between these two extremes there is the possibility of intending the final outcome but discovering how to achieve it. The mode of strategic management here is visionary and ideological. The practical question relates to the part of the spectrum that provides the most useful model for the design of effective strategic actions.

Many would agree that it is virtually impossible to form organisationally intended strategies, but most believe that the future state to which the organisation is moving can, and must be, organisationally intended. There must be a vision if a corporation is to succeed.

ORGANISATIONAL INTENTION AS IDEOLOGY – SHARED VISIONS AND VALUES

It was during the 1980s that the concept of ideology as the driving force of strategic direction came to be widely accepted in business. The idea caught on very rapidly and nowadays one piece of research after another produces the conclusion that it is shared visions and values which are the prime generators of successful patterns in sequences of actions over long time periods, that is, strategies. Prescriptions for success nowadays almost always include the overriding need for leaders with vision and managers who strongly share core values. The terms are firmly established in the vocabulary of managers themselves.

But these terms are used in many different senses, leading to confusion in the actions managers are trying to design. It is therefore a matter of practical importance to be clear on what they mean.

In discussions about ideology, a number of different words are used, often interchangeably, to denote much the same range of concepts. In addition to vision and values, there is the dream, the mission, the strategic intent or purpose, as well as the business philosophy, the culture, the company recipe, the mental model, the frame of reference, the organisation's retained memory. There seem to be three different concepts that these words seek to describe. Sometimes one of the words is used to cover all three concepts. Sometimes different words are used to label each different concept, but not consistently from one person to another. Frequently the words are used so loosely that it is not clear what concept they refer to. The three concepts have to do with what we might call:

1. the future state of the business. This identifies the destination of the business – a pattern of what is to be;
2. the drivers of business behaviour over time. This concept expresses the principal motivators of people in the business – a pattern of becoming;
3. the business philosophy and culture. This is the set of shared beliefs around what the business is there for, what it is, why it is as it is, what makes it successful. It is a set of shared assumptions on how people in the business should behave – a pattern of being.

Consider each of these meanings and the processes that produce them.

The future state of the business

The first sense in which 'vision' and related words are used has to do with what the business is to be at some point in the long-term future. This is purpose in the sense of a reasonably fixed, unique destination. It is purpose as direction into the future; a pattern in what is to be; what it is we want to achieve. Those who prescribe this as the first step in effective strategic management, talk in terms of some realistic future state representing a desirable improvement over the present; a state that has never existed before. It is the future managers wish to create. It provides the overarching goal of the business in the sense that it covers and governs how all the most important issues confronting the organisation are to be dealt with. It must be shared by all managers in a stable manner over time. It is to be questioned and challenged, but only at the margin. It must be specific enough to act, but general enough to allow bold initiative. It is a unanimous, unique answer to the question: 'what will we be in the future?'

How are such visions formed and how do they come to be shared? It is said to be the prime role of the leaders of an organisation to form a vision. They are to do this by listening to those around them, observing what is going on, using clues as to how the world around them will change. It is an intellectual exercise based on some analysis, but it is also intuitive in the sense of a creative leap of the imagination. Vision comes to be shared because leaders preach their vision. Through charisma and discussion, they enrol and gain the enthusiastic commitment of others to that vision.

The proposition, then, is that successful companies are driven by organisational intention taking the form of a vision of the future. On this view, before they choose what to do and then act, key groups of managers in successful companies form a unique, overarching picture of a future state (shape and position of the business related to a market situation). This is a general, qualitative picture that all managers share strongly in a stable way over time. Having formed it, managers do not question it, other than around the edges.[6] Those managers then choose and act in a manner governed by this vision – they do so in an exploratory way, so that the pattern in actions to achieve the future state (the strategy) emerges over time. They search for the route to the vision as they act. But the future state itself is decided in advance, providing intentional direction for the company.

Example 1: Federal Express

Fred Smith is said to have envisioned a future in which letters and small parcels would be delivered overnight across the US by a private enterprise. Fred Smith is said to have envisioned a system consisting of air transport from dispersed collection depots to a central sorting hub where items would be re-routed to delivery depots, the spokes of the hub. The realisation of this 'hub and spoke' vision was Federal Express, and it created a whole new market.

But was Federal Express really a result of so specifically formulated a vision of a future state that was then realised? The answer is no, on two counts.

First, it is a myth that the delivery system concept sprang full-blown from the head of its founder. Some of the original ideas that were to be realised as Federal Express were expounded by Fred Smith in a college paper in 1964, but it took years to develop the concept as a whole. Fred Smith's first business venture after college was that of selling and repairing aircraft. This had little to do with overnight parcel deliveries, but he continued to think about that concept and in 1971 he began to develop it. He bought two jets and set up Federal Express to deliver cheques for the Federal Reserve system, but the Fed backed out of the contract. Despite this he commissioned market research on parcel movements and purchased twenty three additional aircraft. Between 1971 and 1972 he lobbied the air transport regulation authorities to allow the use of his aircraft for parcel deliveries. He and his team also had to expend much effort on raising the finance. It was in 1972 that the 'hub and spoke' design of the delivery system was decided. The first deliveries in a test network covering 11 cities were made in 1973. It was 1976 before the operation made a profit.[7]

Second, Fred Smith did not foresee anything about a future state. What he observed was a current situation. He observed an existing industry for delivering letters and parcels that was fragmented, ineffective, expensive and over regulated. He gathered information on current delivery volumes and how they were currently made. Over time he developed creative ideas on how delivery activities might be improved. He displayed great determination and took big risks in demonstrating that his ideas could work. But he did not foresee anything about the future state in which those ideas would work. He had no idea in advance of whether they would work or not. He had to find this out by doing it. Nothing he did required a picture of a future state.

What actually happened was not as simple as forming a vision of the future and then realising it. These events can be interpreted in another way. There was an initial idea to do with parcel deliveries, but no one knew what shape that would take or whether any given shape would work. Instead of a picture of a future state, there was a provocative idea and a challenge. Fred Smith and his colleagues dealt with a changing agenda of issues and challenges over time provoked by observing current problems and forming ideas on how to deal with them. The issues related to the design of a more effective delivery system, the challenge of air transport regulations, the sources of finance. As they handled these issues, often in a piecemeal fashion without an overarching picture of a future state to guide them, they were learning whether their ideas would work or not. And from that learning emerged the concept that was to be Federal Express. They were discovering both the pattern that was to be and how to secure it – both were emerging.

In this emergent interpretation, it is only with the benefit of hindsight that we are able to detect causal links between some intention and what subsequently happened. When we use hindsight in this way we make what happened seem more organisationally intended than it actually was. And we have a strong tendency to do this because we start with a frame of reference that leads us to look for causal connections even though they may not be there. We have a strong tendency to find stable and regular patterns. The usual way of recounting the Federal Express story could well be subject to interpretive bias.

And the suspicion about this interpretive bias is strengthened when we consider 'visions' that failed. Later, Fred Smith had another vision. This time it was a future state in which Federal Express leased out Zapmail fax machines to customers linked into an expensive and complex satellite telecommunications system. Many millions of dollars later the venture failed as cheap fax machines linked into existing telecommunications networks swept the market. Here it was rivals in another industry that created a new market.

This episode is not usually quoted as a 'vision' on the part of Federal Express. In the case of the first 'vision' it turned out to be beneficial that managers shared it and pursued it with unquestioning determination, if this is indeed what they did. In the case of the second vision the same behaviour led to disaster. In neither case did the managers involved have a picture of a future state enabling them to know in advance what would lead to success and what would not. In both cases they had to learn as they went along.

Example 2: Amstrad

Another noted visionary, this time in the UK, is Alan Sugar who built up a major electronics business, Amstrad, within a few years. His biography does not provide any evidence of some overarching vision of a new electronics company located in some foreseen market state. What it does describe is a man with an ever-changing agenda of issues which he pursued. At one time the issue was that of providing cheap plastic covers for record turntables, then it was integrated tower system hi fi sets, car entertainment systems, personal computers and satellite dishes. And accompanying all these successes, the biographer mentions many issues pursued for a time and then dropped because they were not successful. The biography makes it clear that the shape of the Amstrad business was not foreseen; it evolved as its founder and his colleagues pursued the discovery of opportunities and mistakes with determination and creativity. They were learning through what they did and so discovering their future state.[8]

Cause and effect links

These examples demonstrate that it is not sufficient to prescribe a 'vision' as a prime cause of success – the picture of a future state must, in some sense, be the right one. Anyone can have a fantasy or dream. To be more than this, a picture of a future state has to be anchored to reality. If it is to be useful as a vision, it must say something reasonably specific about the future shape and position of the business in a future market. There must be causal links between a business shape, the market it is to operate in and the performance it is to achieve. There must also be causal links between this future state and the actions required to reach it. These causal links back to action may not be clear cut and direct, as they must be if we are to plan, but they must at least provide criteria for trial and error search, for the means to achieve that picture. If you simply select some picture of a future state and then find that the links back to action are lost in detailed complexity, it will be a matter of pure chance whether you reach that future state or not. You will not be able to say that the organisation as a whole intended it.

These requirements for realism and causal links amount to one of predictability – it must be possible to predict the long-term future outcomes of actions in at least a probabilistic way if there is to be any point in fixing a vision of a future outcome in the first place.

But if the future state is predictable, then competent competitors will no doubt be able to predict it too. The vision will not then be the unique picture prescribed by the ideological mode of strategy formation. There is a straightforward contradiction between the requirement for predictability and that for uniqueness.

If predictability is not possible, and it is because of this belief that the ideological mode prescribes trial and error search rather than a plan, then the prescription to form a vision amounts to the following: select a unique picture of a future state, without knowing whether it will succeed or not; share that vision and cling to it in a determined manner; and then take a chance. This is highly dangerous advice. It is clearly so if the vision turns out to have been wrong. It is even so if the vision turns out to have been right; for what this kind of unquestioning clinging to a successful vision promotes is precisely the kind of excessive concentration on what originally led to success that Miller and Pascale[9] conclude leads ultimately to failure. This point was discussed in Chapter 2.

The point being made is twofold. The first relates to the possibility of forming a useful picture of a future state in the first place. The second relates to the advisability of managers all sharing the same vision and clinging to it over time.

The possibility of forming an operationally useful picture of a future state

The possibility of forming a picture of a future state depends upon the possibility of predicting in some way. Since it recognises that reasonably accurate quantitative forecasting is not possible in turbulent business environments, the ideological approach substitutes a more general qualitative forecast. The idea is that if we cannot control direction to a quantitatively specific point, we can control direction to a reasonably specific qualitative point. We can still be in control of the long-term outcomes of our business actions.

The discoveries about nonlinear dynamics lead us to question this possibility. A business is a nonlinear feedback system and to be continually innovative it has to operate in a state of bounded instability. These points were made in Chapter 3. When a system operates in the area of bounded instability, its long-term future is completely unpredictable in specific terms. There is a lack of clear cut cause and effect links due to the fact that small changes escalate into virtuous and vicious circles. The structure of the system is such that we cannot establish specific enough links between what we do and the outcome of our action, to know what that outcome will be in specific terms. Therefore we cannot intervene in the operation of that system to produce an intended specific outcome. We cannot control the specific long-term outcome.

All we can know about the long-term future of such a system is that it will display familiar, recognisable patterns of a qualitative kind. Does this enable us to fix a qualitative forecast we can then use to control the outcome of our interventions in the business system? The answer is no, because the important point is not whether the future state we want to achieve is quantitatively specific or qualitatively general. The problem lies with the weak links between cause (our action) and effect (the outcome of our action).

Take the weather system as an example. This is a system operating in conditions of bounded instability, so we cannot intervene to change the weather in a specific way. We cannot intervene to produce an extra three inches of rainfall next month because we cannot know what the rainfall would have been without our intervention. But we can know that next month is usually, say, one of low rainfall. We can foresee a qualitative pattern of this kind. Could we intervene to make next month a high rainfall one instead? No, because the very nature of the system means that any intervention we make could have escalating consequences leading to self-reinforcing virtuous and vicious circles that we cannot foresee. Instead of a high rainfall month our intervention might provoke a flood or a drought. Because of escalation, that is, weak links between cause and effect, we cannot know the result of our intervention, in either quantitative or qualitative terms, until we have intervened. There will be recognisable general patterns, but we cannot say which ones until the consequences of our intervention have worked themselves out.

In much the same way, neither long-term quantitative objectives nor long-term qualitative visions allow the managers of a firm to control the long-term outcomes of their actions. In a dynamic system of this kind the links between an action and an outcome are too obscure to enable long-term control of outcomes. The dynamics of success are such that forming a picture of a future state is impossible. And even if it were possible by some mystic means, finding a link back from this picture to action required to produce it would be impossible. When the dynamics are highly complex, all we can know is that we will observe general qualitative patterns in the shape and position of the business that we will be able to identify and understand when we see them. We will be able to do this through reasoning by analogy with other patterns already experienced. We will be able, as a result, to develop new mental models to deal with them. We may well be able to say something about these patterns in advance if we can identify the feedback rules that govern the system, but this something will not overcome the weak links between cause and effect. Therefore it is not possible to design actions now with a controlled outcome even of a very general qualitative kind.

An often-quoted example of a vision is that of the Apollo programme. President Kennedy enunciated the vision of 'a man on the moon'. This galvanised the whole American nation into the effort that led to the realisation of the vision. This, however, provides no analogy at all with the open-ended future a business confronts when it makes strategic choices. We know exactly where the moon is for every second of the year. The technology of jet propulsion was understood at the time of Kennedy's moon vision. Those making the decisions and taking the actions to put a man on the moon were operating in a closed change situation. In that instance the future was knowable. It was possible to have visions and to plan the outcomes of actions. The long-term future facing a business is not closed, it is open-ended – the outcomes are unknowable. This crucial distinction means that visions and plans are not possible.

The advisability of sharing a picture of a future state

This brings us to the second point identified above; that of sharing a picture of a future state. When the future is open-ended and unknowable, it is completely inappropriate and highly dangerous for individuals in a group unquestioningly to share the same picture of a future state. Since none of them can know the outcome, since they have to discover that outcome and learn as they act, it is vital that people continually question what they are doing and why they are doing it. It will not be enough to question some commonly held view simply at the margin. Complex learning requires continual questioning of the very fundamentals of what managers are trying to do together.

Research on visions

Why, then, do researchers keep concluding that shared visions are essential to success? First, they may be using the word to mean something other than a picture of a future state – we will turn to these meanings in the next sections. Second, the evidence that visions of future states have anything to do with business success is anecdotal and conditioned by interpretive bias. What we find is a number of case studies and examples that recount particular business successes in terms of some originating vision. These case studies and examples go back in time to look for a vision that might be said to have started the whole venture off and the ensuing sequence of events is then described in terms of vision realisation. When we do this, we first of all ignore 'visions' that failed. Furthermore we ignore other 'visions' that may have existed at the same time, but that were simply dropped as time passed by. In so doing we are selectively interpreting what actually happened and so, not surprisingly, we confirm the importance of visions.

There is little evidence that successful entrepreneurs somehow foresee future states and then proceed to realise them. What we find instead is highly energetic and hard working people with a full agenda of issues that they are pursuing at any one time. And this agenda continually changes through time, with some issues dropping off the agenda after little exploration, others being discontinued after either minor or major failures, and yet others being progressed to the point where successful new strategies emerge. They do not foresee and then realise, they take big risks with little idea of the outcome, sometimes to succeed and create new markets and technologies, sometimes to fail and have to try again. Successful managers have creative challenging ideas, arising from what they experience and observe. They explore these ideas in a determined, open-minded and continually questioning fashion. Because they cannot know the outcome, they take a chance, they bear risk, they are prepared to back their judgments.

The drivers of business behaviour

The second sense in which 'vision' and related words are used is of a motivational kind. This is purpose in the sense of a reason for doing what we are doing, rather than purpose in terms of what we will achieve. It is a pattern of becoming, rather than a pattern in what will be. Why managers do what they do, can be described using words such as inspirations, aspirations, ambitions, hopes, obsessions, inner standards of excellence, ideas, concepts and difficult challenges. These words convey a sense of destiny rather than that of destination implied by the 'future state' use of the word 'vision'. They are about a belief in the ability to create a future without necessarily knowing what it will look like. 'Vision' in this sense is an answer to the questions:

- Why am I doing what I do?
- Why do I want to become something different?
- Why and how do I want to become better?

The meaning here relates to a pattern in becoming, one embodied in the climate, style or spirit of the organisation. The important point is that people do not have to form a picture of a future state to be driven by 'vision' in its meaning of ambiguous, stretching challenges.

Many examples are given of these drivers of behaviour in a business. Apple is said to be driven by a desire to provide computing for the masses. Ford was driven by the challenge of bringing transport to the masses and Coca Cola by the aspiration to 'put a Coke in arms' reach of everyone'. Polaroid's challenge was to develop instant photography. Other examples of challenges or ambitions relate to rivals – Xerox's desire to 'beat Canon' and Komatsu's obsession to 'encircle Caterpillar'. Yet other examples are provided by Honda's aspiration to become the second Ford and to be an automotive pioneer; or NEC's ambition to acquire technologies to be the best. Global success or unquestioned superiority may be what drives others.

These challenges in reality amount to strong desires to excel at the competition game: to win. The ambitions themselves are usually simple, but important, restatements of the rules of the competitive game, or distillations of the operating recipes of successful entrepreneurs. So Komatsu's 'Encircling Caterpillar' is simply a statement about competing effectively, about winning. In Chapter 2 an example was given of a business seeking to formulate a vision to differentiate itself from its competitors. The proposed vision was that of the company as 'The Innovators'. In this case too, the vision is simply a restatement of a rule all have to follow if they are to succeed. All companies have to strive to win and all companies have to be innovative in today's environment if they are to win.

The proposition put forward by the ideological approach to strategy formation is that successful companies are those where people have the same strong, overarching aspiration in a stable manner over time. They do not question it, other than at the margin. This is part of what provides the focus for their individual efforts and provides purpose for the organisation as a whole. The concern is with cohesion and stability. The prescription is for leaders to set clear organisational aspiration and enrol others to share that aspiration. Aspirations and inspirations are intentionally set by the top level of management.

Generating many different challenges

However, when we see a business organisation as a dynamic feedback system needing to operate in bounded instability to be continually innovative, another perspective is evident. In order continually to learn in turbulent environments where outcomes are unknowable, managers have to keep generating and exploring many different challenges. Those challenges will inevitably be ambiguous and stretching when the consequences of change are unknowable; when many of the changes are small and difficult to detect. In these circumstances problems and opportunities will be ill-structured and difficult to frame. Conflict around how to interpret the challenge, around appropriate ambitions and aspirations, will be inevitable. Indeed such conflict, and the dialogue it ideally leads to, will be required to surface the challenges and explore them. In these circumstances it will be detrimental for leaders to fix on some single aspiration, or some small set of them, for lengthy periods. It will be disadvantageous to the complex learning required if all share the same aspiration.

The dynamic systems view leads to prescriptions of many changing challenges that are ambiguous and stretching, not some obsessively shared aspiration. The challenges generated by complex dynamic systems in open-ended situations emerge from the political interactions between managers and from what and how they are learning together. On this view their role at the top is not to provide simple clear aspirations and then preach them, but to create a context favourable to complex learning, from which challenges may emerge. Those challenges have to do with here and now opportunities and problems, to do with where we have come from and how, not some future state.

This leads to a different view of intention in an organisation. Instead of intention to secure something relatively known and fixed, it is intention to discover what, why and how to achieve. It arises, not from what we foresee, but from what we have experienced and now understand. It is intention to be creative and deal with what comes. Consensus around a particular challenge will sometimes form for a time, but in a continually innovative organisation it will soon be superseded by another. When researchers examine a business they may detect consensus around quality and conclude that it is this 'vision' that is leading to success. If they return some time later they may observe consensus around beating a particular competitor. It all depends on what is the most pressing issue perceived by managers at the time.

From a dynamic system perspective we come to see both vision in its future form, and vision in its form of obsessively shared aspiration, as harmful. These views are too restrictive and if people believe them, they cut out new perspectives. A concern with vision leads us to impose order where this is not what is required. It leads us to think in terms of adapting, not creating. Instead of vision as a future state or a shared aspiration, the dynamic view focuses on ever-changing agendas of issues, aspirations, challenges and ambitions. It focuses on learning and questioning, on difference, ambiguity, contention and creative tension, not the stability and harmony of shared vision. We see success as closely related to continuing states of non equilibrium, instead of states of continuing stable equilibrium and harmony.

Consider now the third sense in which 'vision' and related words are used – the business philosophy or culture.

The business philosophy

The philosophy of any business is a set of beliefs to do with why people in the business are doing what they are doing, and where they are doing it. It incorporates the purpose of the business in the sense of its reason for being. It is the purpose story of the business; its sense of mission. The concept includes the moral standards of the business, the norms relating to the manner in which people within the business should treat each other and how they should treat those outside the business. It is basically the answer to the questions; What am I? Why am I this way? It is a pattern of being. This is much the same as the firm's culture, its retained memory, its recipe, the mental models or frames of reference, that people within the business use to interpret what is happening around them. The words most used in this regard are mission, values and culture.

For example, the business philosophy or culture of IBM is described in terms of 'Service'. The philosophy of Peoples' Express ran in terms of 'People care'. The culture of Marks and Spencers focuses on 'Quality'. The culture will condition how managers approach decision making; how they view the importance of hierarchy; and how they interrelate and act. In some firms decision making is seen as an institutionalised, expert function determined by hierarchical level. In others it may be believed that decisions are better taken after much informal discussion where hierarchical level is not all that important.

The proposition presented by the ideological mode of strategy formation is that successful companies are those having a strongly shared set of cultural values and business philosophies. Such culture and philosophy is appropriate to the future state the firm is trying to reach and to the kind of aspiration required for people to achieve it. The prescription is that cultures can and should be changed to fit what the firm is trying to achieve. Leaders are once again ascribed a prominent role in developing appropriate cultural values. The techniques of organisational development are built on the assumption that it is possible to install and change cultures in an intentional, predetermined manner, at least within limits.

This heavy emphasis on strongly shared cultural values is the main instrument for securing cohesion and maintaining stability in what might otherwise become an unstable system. If power is widely dispersed and people are involved in everything, the whole system could move off in highly uncoordinated ways, unless everyone believes in the same thing. Common value systems will counteract these tendencies and give everyone a sense of belonging. In this requirement the ideological view is little different from the planning one. Common culture and team cohesion is also a prime requirement in that model. There, however, stability was also maintained by clear hierarchies and concentrated power. In the ideological view, common cultures have to bear the main burden of maintaining stability.

Recognition of the important conditioning and stabilising role of culture in an organisation has led to the widespread concern with developing mission statements. These are essentially attempts to encapsulate and communicate the chief tenets of the culture, to provide a focus for change and to spread commitment to desired cultural norms throughout the organisation. But those attempting culture change and mission manufacturing activities are becoming increasingly disillusioned by the poor results achieved.[10] Those results are not surprising when one considers how cultures develop.

A culture is a set of beliefs or assumptions that a group of people share in common on how to view things, how to interpret events, what it is valid to question, what answers are acceptable, how to behave towards others and how to do things. The culture of a group of people develops as they associate with each other. Each person in the group learns to behave and even think in certain ways through the experience of what works and does not work in terms of obtaining the approval or assistance of other members of the group. Groups of people develop distinctive cultures through interaction and the forces applied to any individual to conform become very powerful. It usually takes either insensitivity or courage to be different and yet try to remain in the group.

Strong sharing

This sharing of group culture takes place at different levels. Norms may be shared at an apparent level or at an unconscious level. When we share norms at an apparent level, we conform superficially. We may wear the right clothes, perform the right acts and say the right things without necessarily believing them. Such sharing is obvious. We are aware of it and we can change relatively easily what it is we are sharing. When we share culture at an apparent level that sharing is weak. When a group of people have lived or worked together for some time they inevitably also share norms at an unconscious level. These are matters of conduct, ways of performing and modes of thinking that are simply taken for granted.

We do not have to display them to each other. We do not have to communicate about them. We simply all do them. When cultural sharing occurs at an unconscious level, then it is strongly shared.

However, it takes a long time for such strong sharing to develop. The point is that it cannot be intentionally installed or manufactured in some statement issued by top management. It can only emerge from the continued interaction between people in a group. And once it is shared, the power of conformity makes it extremely difficult to change. Some form of propaganda on its own will simply not be enough to effect change.

The great advantage of strong sharing is that it cuts down on the need to communicate. It speeds up group action and it creates strong cohesion. The great disadvantage is that the assumptions made by everyone in the group are very rarely questioned. Indeed it will usually take some courage to question them at all. This means that in turbulent times they can quickly and disastrously become out of date. Strongly shared cultures inevitably block new learning and cut down on the variety of perspectives brought to bear in any situation. Prime examples of organisations with strong sharing of cultural norms are well established religious orders. Their strong ideologies do not allow for much change. While this may be entirely appropriate for a religious order, it is the opposite of what is required for a business operating in turbulent times.

Those presenting the ideological mode recognise this and therefore prescribe a culture that loves change. But to talk about a strongly shared culture, one of the norms of which is a love of change, is a contradiction in terms. When norms are strongly shared they are shared at an unconscious level. That, by definition, means there is a resistance to change. The more norms we strongly share, the more, by definition, we resist changing them. If we are strongly sharing a norm to change, we cannot then be strongly sharing other norms because that would block the change. If we love change then we share other norms in a weak sense only – that is what loving change means.

No group can operate effectively in the complete absence of some cultural sharing. In defining what may be appropriate sharing in a business it is helpful to distinguish between what may be called performing and learning cultural norms. Performing norms relate to what a group is doing together in carrying out its day-to-day activities and how they behave towards each other as they do this. Learning norms relate to how they interpret what is going on around them, what it is permissible to question, what answers it is acceptable to give and generally how they think about things. The sharing of both performing and learning norms at the apparent level is necessary for a group to work effectively together. But this is weak sharing. Strong sharing, that is at the unconscious level, of some important performing norms may greatly improve the efficiency of the existing business. For example, norms on what constitutes quality and customer care. But strong sharing of learning norms will always be harmful and even strong sharing of a few performing norms runs risks. Such strong sharing blocks complex learning.

Weak sharing

It was argued in Chapter 3 that feedback systems, such as a business, must operate in conditions of bounded instability to be successful. The absence of strongly shared cultural norms is one of the major characteristics of this dynamic in a business. In this state we get the multiple perspectives required for innovative activity. Weakly shared cultural norms play another important role in the dynamics of a successful business system. They provide boundaries around sequences of choices. If everyone strongly shares the same culture, they may well pursue the same sequence of choices for lengthy periods of time with possibly disastrous consequences. If members of a group share nothing in terms of culture, they will all move endlessly in different directions. If however, cultural sharing takes a weak form, the group will be able to work together, but they will not be able to pursue the same sequence of choices for lengthy periods. Some members will raise objections, leading to examination of what they are doing. In this way, weak sharing provides important boundaries around instability. There will also be enough contention to break existing patterns of behaviour and current perceptions.

Weakly shared cultural norms do weaken team cohesion. But does a successful work group need to be cohesive? During the Second World War, the behaviour of bomb crews on missions to Germany was studied. Some of the crews constituted cohesive teams. They liked each other and socialised together. Other crews were not cohesive in this sense. The latter performed better. They focused on the task instead of socialising. It seems that groups can work very effectively together without being cohesive. Mutual reliance on each others' contributions and some trust is all that is required. Cohesion creates social groups not work groups.

The dynamic systems perspective leads to a view of culture as emergent. What a group comes to share in the way of culture and philosophy emerges from individual personal beliefs through a learning process that takes time and builds up over years.[11] And if the learning process is to continue, if a business is to be continually innovative, the emphasis should be on questioning the culture not sharing it. A dynamic systems perspective points to the importance of encouraging counter cultures to overcome powerful tendencies to conform and share cultures strongly.

HOW CHAOS WILL LEAD MANAGERS TO THINK AND ACT IN A DIFFERENT WAY

The mental framework most managers adopt today is still one in which there are, in principle, clear connections between causes and effects, so that it is possible to undertake actions to achieve predetermined outcomes. They still think in terms of installing some form of systematic management process to enable top managers to control the future development of the business in terms of outcomes. And they have a very specific view on the meaning of control. That view is one where control is a negative, damping feedback process that keeps the organisation close to a position, a predetermined path, or a direction. There is no place for chance outcomes in the mental frameworks being used. Success is seen as a state of continuing stability, the only alternative to which is explosive instability. Order and disorder are seen as clearly separate opposites, the subject of 'either/or' choice.

The discovery that nonlinear feedback systems are capable of an additional form of behaviour, bounded instability, opens up the possibility of a rather different model of the strategy process. More strongly than that, observation that successful, creative companies display the escalating and self-reinforcing behaviour typical of the state of bounded instability requires an explanation of the strategy process which takes account of chaotic dynamics. And chaotic dynamics mean that the links between action and their outcomes over the long term are lost in the detail of what actually happens. Managers cannot form a vision of some future state towards which the business can then be moved – the futures open to the system are too many and the links between a future and the actions leading to it too obscure. Chaotic dynamics lead us to see strategy as a direction into the future that emerges from what managers do. In chaotic conditions strategy cannot be driven by prior intention. Instead it is the creation of order out of chaos, quite unintended at an overall organisational level.

The dynamic systems perspective then leads managers to think in terms, not of the prior intention of objectives and visions, but of continuously developing agendas of issues, aspirations, challenges and individual intentions. The key to emerging strategy is the effectiveness with which such agendas of issues are continually built and dealt with by managers in an organisation. When they think in terms of dynamic systems, managers will design actions to build and attend to agendas of issues, instead of trying to peer into the future to determine a vision or a long-term objective.

The dynamic systems perspective will alter the actions that managers design in other important respects. The concern for common cultures and cohesive teams will be replaced with actions designed to promote different, counter cultures so as to continually generate new perspectives and place boundaries around sequences of choices. Instead of designing flexible structures managers will design structures which are as simple and clear as possible. They will see structure as the control instrument relevant to short interval rather than strategic control. Instead of trying to empower people by encouraging widespread participation and more equal power distribution, managers will be concerned with how power is being used, what impact this has on group dynamics and thus on how effectively key groups of managers in the organisation are learning together. It is this learning activity which is the key to developing effective strategies.

When we interpret the strategy formation process from the dynamic systems perspective we think about emergent strategies in a different way. The new frame of reference leads us to ask how we can intend, not the specific pattern of action that is a strategy, but the effective learning and political behaviour that makes it possible for a pattern to emerge. We see emergence as a process by means of which the business system as a whole can create order out of chaos, through agents in that system interacting, not through a few directing the others in a centrally intended manner. Strategies do not emerge no matter what we do, they may emerge if we learn effectively together. Strategic management is seen then as a learning and political process, having specific outcomes so dependent on the detail of what we and others do that they are unpredictable.

When managers deal with ill-structured, ambiguous issues with unknowable consequences, they display unstable behaviour which we label as conflict, confusion, tension, equivocation, defence routines, cover ups, game playing, avoidance and many more. There are boundaries around, recognisable categories of, that behaviour – but within those categories, the specific sequences of behaviour are always different and unpredictable in terms of decision outcome. This happens because when managers are making decisions in conditions of great uncertainty, they are highly sensitive to the context within which they are doing so. Who is involved in the decision making, how they use their power, what other time pressures are on them, all determine the kind of behaviour they display. And that behaviour has a powerful effect on the decisions they make. Small changes in context can have a major impact on how people behave in a highly uncertain situation and so affect the choice they make. Such sensitivity makes the outcome of their interaction unpredictable. The behaviour of managers when they confront open-ended, that is strategic, situations meets all the criteria of chaos.

And out of this chaos, managers *do* produce order. As groups, they reach periodic consensus around, and commitment to, a particular response to a specific open-ended issue. That response may be the start of an innovation, a new strategic direction. This order of periodic commitment, is of that fragile kind, requiring continuing inputs of energy and attention, that is characteristic of new forms of behaviour produced by far-from-equilibrium systems in nature. When successful managers produce the order of periodic consensus, they are not doing so as a result of central direction, but through a communication process of learning and political interaction that is spontaneous and self-organising. And from this process there emerges a pattern in long-term sequences of actions that are the strategies of the business.

REFERENCES

1. Ries, A & Trout, J (1989) *Bottom-Up Marketing*, McGraw-Hill, Maidenhead.

2. Miller, D & Friesen, P H (1980) 'Momentum and Revolution in Organizational Adaptation', Academy of Management Journal, 23.

3. Quinn, J B (1978) 'Strategic Change: 'Logical Incrementalism'', Strategic Management Review, no 20, Fall.

4. Mintzberg, H & Waters J A (1985) 'Of Strategies Deliberate and Emergent', Strategic Management Journal, vol 6.

5. Pascale, R T (1990) *Managing at the Edge: How Companies use Conflict to Stay Ahead*, Viking Penguin, London.

6. Peters, T (1985) *Thriving on Chaos*, Macmillan, London.

7. Quinn, J B Federal Express Corporation, in J B Quinn, H Mintzberg & R M James, (1988) *The Strategy Process*, Prentice-Hall, Englewood Cliffs, NJ.

8. Thomas, D (1990) *Alan Sugar: The Amstrad Story*, Century, London.

9. See reference to these books in Chapter 2.

10. Campbell, A & Tawady, K (1990) *Mission and Business Philosophy: Winning Employee Commitment*, Heinemann, London.

11. Campbell, A and Tawady, K op. cit.
    Senge, P (1990) *The Fifth Discipline: The Art and Practice of the Learning Organization*, Bantam Doubleday, New York.

7

Strategic Control and Irregularity

Managers today approach the problem of control from two different angles. On the one hand, control is seen as a planning and monitoring activity. This requires clear hierarchies of managers with well defined roles, as well as rules, regulations and procedures governing the allocation of responsibility and authority for achieving objectives. On the other hand, control is seen as ideological in nature. Here control is exercised, not through hierarchies, rules and regulations, but through shared beliefs in a vision and through a common set of values or culture. The former is an essentially structural approach with the consequent advantage of clarity, but the disadvantage of inflexibility. The latter is an essentially behavioural approach with the advantage of flexibility, but the disadvantage of being less governable from the centre. In practice, managers adopt a combination of these two approaches.

But, although they are different in many respects, both of the above angles on control have the same aim and are based on the same unquestioned assumptions. The aim of both the structural and the ideological forms of control is to secure regularity in the pattern of behaviour of the business system as a whole. The point of control in both cases is the adaptation of the organisation to its environment; the establishment of the stable equilibrium organisation. In both cases, control is seen as a negative feedback loop that keeps the organisation moving towards some predetermined, intentional future point. The structural and ideological understandings of control are based on assumptions that the future is predictable to some reasonably useful extent and that the concept of probability is a practically useful one in the change situations confronting a business. These amount to an assumption that there are reasonably close links between causes and their

157

effects, between actions and their outcomes. Both approaches to control assume that the same control philosophy can be applied to the short- and the long-term futures facing the business. Strategic control is not seen as conceptually different to day-to-day control; the former is simply a less precise version of the latter.

What we end up with, then, is a view of control in which some individual, or small group of individuals, is in control of the behaviour of the business system and the outcomes of that behaviour over both the short and the long term. Those at the top set the objectives and establish the rules and hierarchies, or they formulate the vision and define the culture, or they do both. On this view systems for short-term and strategic control are to be installed and centrally directed in some sense.

However, when the behaviour of a business organisation is understood from a dynamic systems perspective, today's received wisdom on the nature of control is relegated to a special case model, applicable primarily to the short-term control of the business. Strategic control has to be understood in completely different terms. This chapter will argue that the long-term future of a dynamic system is unknowable because cause and effect links are lost in the detail of what happens. Consequently, the long-term control of a business has to take a different form to that of the received wisdom. This is a form in which the behaviour of the business system as a whole is controlled, but no individual, or small group of individuals, is in control of that behaviour or its outcomes. The behaviour of the business system as a whole is controlled when political interaction between people in the organisation is effective and when those people undertake learning of a complex type. Political interaction and complex learning in groups are themselves forms of organisational control, even though no individual is in control of them. In open-ended situations controlled behaviour, in a whole organisation sense, emerges from self-organising politics and learning. This kind of control is about creating markets, not adapting to them. It depends upon bounded instability and far-from-equilibrium states, not stability and equilibrium. Control here is an amplifying activity that spreads new perspectives through an organisation. The concern is with patterns in action, or strategies, that are irregular rather than regular because they are new and innovative breaks with the past. Those at the top of the organisation can create the necessary conditions for bounded instability, but they cannot control the outcomes.

What we end up with on this dynamic systems view, is an understanding of control as the simultaneous application of diametrically opposed forms of behaviour. Planning/monitoring forms of control with their inflexible hierarchies and compliant behaviour are essential for effective short interval control of the existing business from day to day. But at the same time, strategic control as self-organising politics and learning must be practised if the business is to develop new direction. This form of control requires the opposite of compliance and it actually threatens the existing day-to-day activities. It generates questioning and contention. Control in total terms is the continual resolution of the tensions created by the need to apply short interval and strategic forms of control, by the opposing pulls of stability and instability.

The need for these two completely different forms of control arises because a business faces completely different types of change situation. Therefore, to develop the argument, this chapter considers first the change situations in which a business has to exercise control. A distinction is drawn between the closed, contained and open-ended changes facing a business. We then consider how different understandings of the nature of control can apply to those different change situations.

THE CHANGE SITUATIONS CONFRONTING DYNAMIC SYSTEMS

Management is fundamentally about handling change. How managers do this has to depend upon the principal characteristics of that change, if their actions are to be effective. What, then, are the principal characteristics of change generated by dynamic systems?

The past

The current state of a dynamic system is a record of everything that has happened to it; everything that the actors or components within it have done in the past. When the system is far-from-equilibrium, its history is important and that history will continue to affect what happens to it in the future. Managers quite clearly recognise this. At the start of every consultancy assignment I have been on, the client managers recount the history of their organisation, so explaining the current situation they find themselves in. Managers and consultants alike recognise that they cannot understand what to do next until they have established some account of what has happened. Board and top executive meetings are often dominated by accounts of what has happened.

Closed change

When we look back at the history of a business, there are some sequences of events which we can recount clearly in a manner that commands the widespread agreement of the managers involved. We are able to say what happened, why it happened and what the consequences were. We are also able to explain in a widely accepted way how such a sequence of events and actions will continue to affect the future course of the business. We can call these closed change situations.

The principal features of closed change are that the consequences of events are clearly understandable in their past form and accurately predictable in their future form. These principal features apply because the events and actions generating the consequences have already occurred and causality is clear cut. This applies to the normal, continuing operation of the existing business. For example, consider a business that supplies pop records and tapes to the teenage market. Managers in that business are able to say with some precision how the number of customers in that market has changed over the past and furthermore how it will change for the next fifteen years or so. Those customers already exist. The managers can establish fairly clear cut relationships between the number of customers and the number of records and tapes they have bought and will buy. Closed change is depicted in Figure 7.1 as the shaded area under curve A. This curve shows how the sequence of actions and events began at some point in the past, time t_{-1} on the horizontal axis, and then how the consequences developed to the present t_0, and will proceed into the future.

Contained change

But other sequences of events and actions flowing from the past are less clear cut. Here we find that we are only able to say what probably

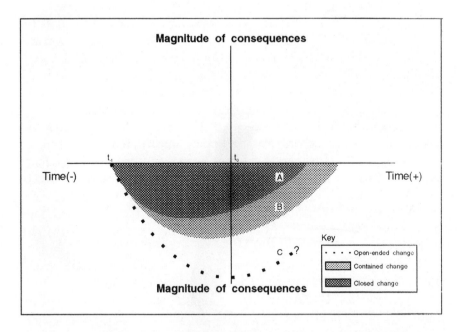

Figure 7.1 The change situations generated by past events and actions

happened, why it probably happened, and what its probable consequences were. The impact of such a sequence of events upon the future course of the business has similarly to be qualified by probability statements. For example, the supplier of records and tapes will find it harder to explain why particular kinds of records and tapes sold better than others. That supplier will find it somewhat difficult to forecast what kinds of tapes and records will sell better in the future. But market research, life style studies and statistical projections will enable reasonably helpful forecasts for at least the short term. Causality is approximate or statistical. It takes the form of probability statements. We can call this kind of change contained. It is represented in Figure 7.1 as the shaded area under curve B.

Open-ended change

And there are yet other sequences of events and actions arising from the past which continue to impact on the future where explanations do not command anything like widespread acceptance by those involved. The company supplying records and tapes may have decided in the past to diversify into video film distribution, by acquiring another company already in that business. That acquisition may now be unprofitable and the managers involved could well subscribe to conflicting explanations of why this is so. Some may claim that the market for video films is too competitive. Others that the diversification was a wrong move because it meant operating in a different market with which they were not sufficiently familiar. Others may say that it is due to a temporary decline in demand and that the market will pick up in the future. Yet others may ascribe it to poor management of the acquisition, or to a failure to integrate it properly into the business, or to a clash of cultures between the two businesses. What that team of managers do next to deal with low profitability obviously depends upon the explanation of past failure they subscribe to.

This kind of change situation may be called open-ended. Here we do not know with any clarity what caused the change, why the change occurred or what its consequences were and will be. It is depicted in Figure 7.1 as the blank area under the dotted curve C. That curve ends with a question mark because the managers do not know what the consequences of the particular sequence of events and actions will be in the future.

The present and the future

As they stand in the here and now, at time t_0 in Figure 7.1, managers face three different kinds of change situation arising from sequences of events and actions that have already occurred. There are also sequences of events and actions that are starting up now, in the present. Some of these will be closed change – an existing customer places a much larger order for an existing product line. Some sequences of events and actions will be contained change – a new customer places orders for a modified range of products. And others will be open-ended change – setting up a new activity in Poland.

Yet other sequences of events and actions will be initiated at future points. Each of these sequences will also have closed, contained and open-ended components. Figure 7.1 is completed in Figure 7.2 by the addition of curves representing these present and future consequences. (The vertical axis measures the magnitude of the consequences without distinguishing between negative and positive. The diagram is drawn this way simply for visual clarity.)

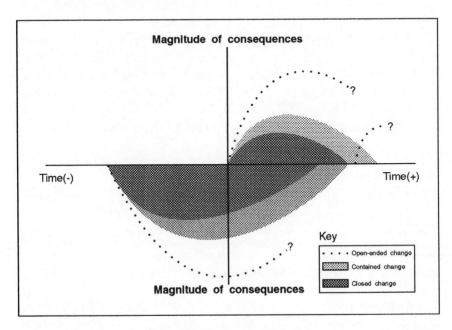

Figure 7.2 The nature of change

The point the diagram makes is this. As they stand in the here and now, managers in any company face a spectrum of change situations in every time frame, from the past through the present to the future. At each point, that spectrum stretches from predictable closed change, through statistically predictable contained change, into unknowable open-ended change. The past and the short-term future are dominated by closed and contained change, but the long-term future is predominantly open-ended.

This pattern of change situations is a consequence of the dynamics of the business system. When the dynamics are chaotic, small changes escalate and self-reinforcing circles develop, making it totally impossible to predict the long-term future outcome of sequences of events and actions. In this sense the long-term future of the system is inherently unknowable, but because it takes time for escalation to occur, it is possible to forecast the short-term future of the system. Closed and contained change relate to developments that have short-term consequences. They are repetitions of what has happened before. They are large numbers of the same kind of event and it is therefore useful in a practical sense to apply probability concepts and statistical techniques to specify their consequences. Open-ended change is unique and has never happened in that specific form before. Measures of probability, therefore, have no practical use in decision making. Simulating the future of the business, or building scenarios of its possible futures will not provide forecasts of the likely range of outcomes. Simulation may be useful but only as a learning or practice exercise to get a feel for the kinds of future patterns which may develop.

Managers cannot choose to focus on one kind of change or another, if they wish to survive. A business will have to deal simultaneously with all forms of change if it wishes to survive and prosper. But because open-ended change is qualitatively different from closed and contained change, it will have to be dealt with in a completely different way.

Behaviour in closed/contained change situations

When change is closed or contained, reasonably clear cut links can be established between causes and effects. Such changes have consequences that can be forecast to a reasonably useful degree of accuracy. This means that the problems and opportunities facing managers are fairly clear. Any difficulties lie in finding the answers, not in identifying the questions to ask in the first place. The situation is not characterised by ambiguity, therefore competent managers do not behave in an equivocal manner. If they conflict, there is a substantial possibility of settling the conflict by rational argument. Failing that, the application of power as authority derived from the clear rules and structures of the organisation can be applied to settle differences. Alternatively, bargains of one sort or another can be used to resolve the conflict. By and large people know what they are doing in closed and contained situations. They will usually have decided what to do before the change occurs. The behaviour of groups of people and the common models they use to design their actions are all understandable and reasonably predictable in these situations.

Behaviour in open-ended change situations

But when managers confront open-ended change the situation is completely different in every respect. They are faced with actions and events past, present and future that have unknowable consequences. Links between cause and effect are lost in the detail of those events because small changes escalate and self-reinforcing circles appear. The key difficulty then is that of identifying what the problems and opportunities are; not that of finding answers, but identifying what questions to ask. The situation is ambiguous and the responses of managers are equivocal. In these unique, new situations, old shared mental models on how to design actions do not work. New mental models have to be developed and shared before anything can happen. Conflict around how to interpret what is going on and how to design actions to deal with it becomes commonplace and inevitable. Such conflict is actually a vital part of developing new mental models. Predetermined rules and authority structures become useless as effective means of settling the conflicts, because they presuppose that someone has made up his or her mind and knows what to do.

The unpredictability of specific events within fuzzy categories, which is the hallmark of open-ended change leads to ambiguity and confusion. Although individual human minds are well equipped to deal with such situations, they are difficult because they require developing new mental models through analogous reasoning. That difficulty is magnified many times when a reasonably common mental model has to be shared by a number of people in the management team before they can take joint action. The manner in which they interact with each other then becomes a vital part of the decision making process they employ. We cannot understand what they decide to do, without understanding the impact of their personalties and the group dynamic. In this change situation, people typically feel insecure and become anxious. The dynamic of the interaction between people in a group becomes much more complex and can quite often be bizarre. There is a strong tendency to apply inappropriate mental models of the learning process.

The key point is this. When the system is chaotic the long-term consequences of actions past, present and future are open-ended, where that means that they are unknowable. They are not simply currently unknown: it is totally impossible to know what they will be. This distinction between the unknown and the unknowable is an important one. If the future is simply unknown there is the possibility that we will be able to identify it, if we gather enough information, conduct enough research and perform enough analysis. If it is unknowable then these things are a waste of time and we need to focus on different ways of doing things.

What do these different change situations mean for the control forms it is possible for managers to apply to their business?

CONTROL FORMS AND CHANGE SITUATIONS

Controlled behaviour is that which has some overall coherence or pattern; that is, behaviour which is internally connected and constrained. It is the opposite of haphazard, unconnected thinking and acting without any pattern on the one hand; or predictable explosively unstable behaviour on the other. The key criteria for control are connectedness, constraint and pattern in action.

Connectedness

For behaviour to be connected there has to be a feedback loop between:

- discovering what is going on or changing;

- making conscious or unconscious choices to respond to, or provoke, changes;

- acting upon those choices; and then

- discovering what the consequences of those actions are, in order to make further choices and take further actions.

These elements of discovery, choice and action must be connected in the sense that choice is based on what is discovered, action flows from choice, and the consequences of action are discovered so as to influence the next choice. It is possible in human behaviour for that feedback connection to break down so that behaviour is uncontrolled. Two people may argue fiercely, but still be controlled, if each consciously or unconsciously discovers the reaction of the other to a statement and then makes the next statement in the light of that discovery. Here people are listening to each other and choosing their next statements on the basis of the response made by the other. Where one simply makes a series of statements, not hearing or understanding the other, we get an uncontrolled argument that is either haphazard and meaningless or explodes into a quarrel.

All controlled behaviour must follow a connected feedback loop, but it is possible to define the elements of that loop (discovery, choice and action) in different ways. And the difference between closed/contained change and open-ended change is so great that we have to define the elements of control in different ways. Dramatically different change situations require very different forms of control.

Constraint

In addition to connected feedback, control requires the presence of some form of constraint to prevent behaviour from becoming explosively unstable. For an organisation, we normally see that constraint as being provided by some form of shared organisational intention. It may be an end point all are striving for; it may be a path they all agree to follow; it may be a set of rules they all agree (or are compelled) to obey. This form of constraint requires central direction and mechanisms for securing agreement or acceptance. It leads to negative feedback control. But we do not have to define constraint in this way and indeed in open-ended change we cannot.

Pattern

Negative feedback regulates the behaviour of a system – it produces a regular and therefore repetitive pattern of actions and consequences. But controlled behaviour could also take the form of irregular patterns. For example, the weather system produces controlled behaviour, but weather patterns are irregular. Controlled business behaviour in open-ended change situations also produces irregular rather than regular patterns.

Consider how each of these properties of connectedness, constraint and pattern apply in different change situations to produce different forms of control.

Planning and monitoring forms of control in closed and contained situations

The elements of the feedback control loop (discovery, choice and action) can be defined precisely and operated in a negative feedback manner to produce regular patterns in action, only when the changes are closed or contained. In closed or contained situations, the consequences of change are predictable; there is a clear link between cause and effect. Control can therefore be practised in its negative feedback forms as planning. In planning forms of control, behaviour is connected in that there are clearly laid out steps from discovery as formal, analytical scanning of the environment; to choice as objective setting and plan formation; to action as plan implementation and then back through formal monitoring to discovery again. Here, behaviour is constrained by organisational intention relating to objectives and planned routes to them. And the pattern of action produced is a regular planned movement to the objective. All of this is possible because the change situation is closed or contained.

This control loop is depicted in Figure 7.3. Behaving in a planned manner means going around the control loop which connects precisely defined discovery, choice and action through time. The ability to do this depends critically on the possibility of establishing causal links running from patterns in actions to the future shape and position of the business; and from future shape and position to future performance.

Ideological form of control in closed and contained situations

In the ideological model of control, the connections run from discovery as informal listening and observation; to choice as a vision; to action as trial and error experiments; and back to discovery again through learning about the outcomes of action. As with the planning and monitoring form of control, there is feedback connection between discovery, choice and action – the definitions are simply different.

In the ideological form of control, behaviour is constrained by the ideology itself and by the criteria for trial and error action. The ideology consists of an overarching organisational vision or intention which all are inspired to follow, accompanied by the strong sharing of core cultural

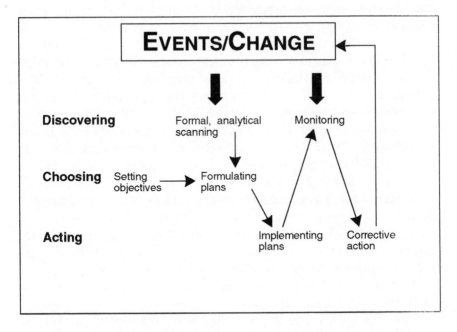

Figure 7.3 Planning/monitoring control in closed/contained situations

values throughout the organisation. The ideology also provides criteria for the selection of trial actions as does the principle of focus, namely that trial actions should constitute a logically incremental move from the existing core business.

This trial and error form of control depends upon the laws of large numbers, or probability. The idea is that large numbers of random shocks, or unforeseeable changes, keep hitting the firm. If that firm undertakes large numbers of mostly random, small trial actions, then by the laws of large numbers, some will match some of the random shocks in the sense of being appropriate responses. On the other hand many will not. But, because of the large numbers involved, the inappropriate responses will tend to cancel out. Provided that the firm acts faster than its rivals, provided that it produces more random trials to counter the random shocks, it will succeed according to the laws of probability. Trial and error action as a form of control depends upon the occurrence of large numbers of the same events within each of a given number of categories. For example, this happens when we toss a coin – the results, over and over again, are heads or tails. Such control produces a more irregular pattern in action, but nevertheless, one of movement to a predetermined destination.

But when a dynamic system operates in conditions of bounded instability, no specific event is ever repeated in exactly the same way. The probability of any specific event occurring, therefore, is infinitely small. At critical points in the development of a dynamic system when it is far-from-equilibrium, the laws of probability cannot be said to apply in any practical way. Then, each specific event is unique, falling only into general qualitative categories of the family resemblance type. And in business you do not typically get a large number of chances to repeat events which bear a family resemblance close enough to apply probability in even an approximate way.

So, when the dynamic is complex, when the change is open-ended, there is no guarantee that trial and error mismatches with random environmental shocks will cancel out. Large numbers of random actions, even within boundaries set by logical connection with the existing business and core values cannot be relied upon as search techniques that will take the business to its intended vision. The ideological form of control requires a causal connection between the vision and the actions required to realise it. It can therefore only be applied in closed and contained change situations.

Planning and ideological forms of control have the same aim

The ideological approach puts forward a very different mechanism for control, when compared to the long-term planning approach. But both approaches seek to do the same thing: they are both concerned with the intentional adaptation of the business to its environment. Both see success as flowing from the maintenance of order and stability. The one secures order through hierarchy, formal rules, procedures and analytical techniques. The other secures order through ideology and belief. Both proclaim that a system of some sort, analytical or ideological, can be installed to secure success. Such a system allows the top executives of the business to be in control of the outcome of strategic activity. Both propose a negative feedback form of control in which the business is kept to a predetermined path of some sort. The dynamic for both is the drive to equilibrium adaptation in which there are clear connections between cause and effect, even though we may not always be aware of what those connections are. Both are concerned with producing regular patterns in behaviour. And both can apply only to closed and contained change situations.

Learning and political interaction in open-ended situations

For a complex dynamic system, control in its planning/monitoring and ideological forms is only possible in the short term. In the open-ended change which applies to the long term, the elements of the control loop cannot be precisely defined, nor can they operate in a negative feedback way. The control loop has to take the form of continual learning and political interaction in real time. This form of control and development has already been discussed in Chapter 4 (for the figure depicting the control loop, see page 88 and compare with Figure 7.3 on page 169).

This loop constitutes a form of control because it is one of feedback connection between discovery, choice and action. Behaviour generated by this loop can be constrained and produce a pattern. The constraint and the pattern are provided by the nature of chaos, or bounded instability itself. Chaotic behaviour is a form of controlled behaviour.

An important insight provided by the modern science of dynamic systems is that negative feedback leading to stable regularity is not the only form of control. A nonlinear feedback system may generate chaotic behaviour and this is constrained, or bounded, even though it is also unstable. There are general, qualitative, patterns in chaotic behaviour, even though these patterns are irregular and their specifics are random. The boundaries are provided by the nonlinear structure of the system itself; they are not centrally directed or agreed in a prior way by the components of the system. This is a self-organising, amplifying form of behaviour which is nevertheless controlled because it has pattern, it is constrained and it is connected because it is a feedback loop. It is discovering, choosing and acting in a connected manner. But it is responding to change by amplifying that change to form different patterns of behaviour, nevertheless falling into recognisable categories. It is a creative, non equilibrium form of control, not the repetitive stabilising form that negative feedback produces. No agent within the system can control the outcome, but the behaviour of the system is still controlled. This is what managers are doing when they interact politically and when they perform complex learning in groups.

Note that central, shared intention is not an essential requirement for there to be controlled behaviour. We can intend explosive instability and that is not controlled. Behaviour may be chaotic, without central shared intention, and yet it is controlled. Predictability and stability are also not essential requirements for control. Explosive instability follows a perfectly predictable course and yet it is not controlled. Chaotic behaviour is unpredictable and unstable, but still controlled.

Learning as control

People learning in a group are displaying controlled behaviour. There are connections running from the discovery by individuals of small changes, anomalies and ambiguities; to choice arising out of reflection, contention and dialogue around the issues being discovered; to exploratory action; and back to discovery again as the processes of choice and the outcomes of exploratory actions provide further prompts to individual discoveries. Here behaviour is constrained partly by individual differences in culture and perceptions; by disagreements preventing a single view from dominating. Behaviour is also partly constrained by the shared views that groups working together come to acquire, but constantly have to question if they are to learn. Constraint then is a consequence of the tension between sharing and difference. The extremes of sharing and difference both remove the constraints and lead to uncontrolled behaviour.

Politics as control

People interacting politically are also displaying controlled behaviour. Connection runs from discovery as the formation of individual and sub-unit issues; to choice as the building of support through persuasion and negotiation, the application of power; to action; and back to discovery again as action generates yet other issues. Behaviour is constrained by the unequal distribution of power, by the existence of hierarchy, by the need to sustain sufficient support for the progress and enaction of issues.

An example of political activity as a form of control is provided by the removal of Prime Minister Thatcher from office in the UK in 1991. This powerful figure gradually lost support around the issues of the UK's relationship with the European Community and the matter of the poll tax. Opposition groups formed covertly. One of these crystallised around Heseltine and became overt. A somewhat ambiguous support group formed around Thatcher, but within it there were factions, one supporting Major as an alternative and another supporting Hurd. On the first ballot Thatcher did not secure enough votes, by a very small margin. At first she intended to go to a second ballot, but then, apparently on the advice of a small number of people, she withdrew. Major won on the second ballot.

Here the outcome was unpredictable; events unfolded. But with hindsight there was a pattern to be seen in the way coalitions formed and shifted. Behaviour was contained and connected. No one centrally directed the formation of the factions and coalitions that determined the final result. The process was not driven by a plan or a shared culture; it was differences in views and values that were driving the process. What those involved were doing was amplifying and spreading views in a destabilising manner. A small difference from the required vote in the first ballot had escalating consequences. But throughout, behaviour was constrained by the need to sustain support – it was controlled although no one was individually controlling it. Much the same process occurs around many issues in a business. It is not as obvious because the process is not played out on a media stage. Therefore it is often not examined or even perceived to be the control process that is being applied.

Amplifying control

In learning and political interaction, control amplifies rather than damps, but amplifies within boundaries. In both cases, issues and perspectives are being spread through the organisation, challenging existing patterns and therefore destabilising the organisation. That instability is essential to the development of the new, but it is constrained. Control has to take the form of individuals and groups within the organisation learning and politically interacting in real time, but within boundaries. Learning and political interaction is behaviour that is as coherent and controlled as planning and vision fulfilment – the process is simply different, the definitions of the elements in the loop are simply different, connectedness and constraint simply take different forms appropriate to the change situation in which control is to be exercised.

Top management also exerts an influence on the learning and political form of coherent behaviour that is just as important as the influence it exerts through plans and visions – the area of influence is simply different. Instead of influencing through fixing intentions and establishing predetermined rules to yield an outcome, top management exerts its influence in open-ended change by operating on the boundary conditions surrounding the learning process in the organisation. In open-ended change there can be no central control over the choices made or their outcomes. But through operating on the boundary conditions, top managers determine whether learning occurs at all, how widespread that learning is and what quality it displays. Those boundary conditions have to do with the manner in which power is used, the group dynamic it provokes, the culture of the group and the time pressures it faces.

Since a successful business system is one where continuing, prior, shared intention is impossible; patterns in action are essentially irregular; and relationships with the environment are creatively interactive; there can be no template against which to control. Long-term control as a damping feedback activity is impossible.

Damping, or negative feedback, as a form of control is a concept appropriate to systems operating in stable equilibrium states. Here control performs the task of keeping the system's development over time close to its stable equilibrium state. Where we need a system to continually perform the same tasks in a reliable manner, then we need damping controls to sustain stable equilibrium. It is a great misfortune when the human heart moves away from its stable equilibrium state into a chaotic one – the result is a heart attack. We do not want a country's electricity system to operate in any state other than stable equilibrium. There are some human systems that most of us desire to see in stable equilibrium – most do not want religious organisations to display the bounded instability that may lead them to be continually innovative.

But business organisations are different. They constitute human feedback systems that must continually innovate if they are to survive. To do so they have to operate away from equilibrium in the area of bounded instability. Here development is not restrained by controls of a damping feedback kind. Instead, development is characterised by amplifying feedback within boundaries. The system develops by amplifying small changes. And this can be seen in innovative organisations when champions fasten on to some issue, build support for it, and so possibly turn it into a new direction for the company. In other words, the control process is a political one with amplifying characteristics. The boundaries around this process are provided by the existence of power and the need to build and retain political support. The other concept of control which we do not normally apply to business organisations is the political process. In innovative organisations it operates in an amplifying manner.

HOW CHAOS WILL LEAD MANAGERS TO THINK AND ACT IN A DIFFERENT WAY

The open-ended change which flows from chaotic dynamics is such that there is no clear cut link between a limited number of causes and an effect. It follows that we cannot specify an intention and then identify a limited number of events and actions that will lead to fulfilment of that intention. Instead, consequences emerge or unfold in a manner dependent upon the precise detail of all the many small events that occur and actions that are taken. So, when managers are confronted by open-ended change, they cannot practise a form of control that requires prior, overarching organisational intention. Top management cannot practise a centralised form of organisational control that relies upon setting predetermined rules and routes for individuals within the organisation to follow, against which their conduct can be monitored. Control as we normally think of it in business, that is as negative, or damping, feedback sustaining equilibrium, is not a possibility in open-ended change – the strategic. It is a concept of control applicable only to closed and contained change situations – the short term day-to-day.

But this does not mean that there can be no form of strategic control. It means that we have to think about control in a more general sense. The behaviour of a business organisation as a whole may be controlled in a general sense, even though no agent within or outside it is able to control, in the sense of determining, the specific outcomes of its behaviour.

If our understanding of how feedback mechanisms operate is one in which the choice is between stability on the one hand or explosive instability on the other, then the only state to strive for must be stability.

We will then see control entirely in terms of negative feedback to secure regularity and stability. We will define the discovering, choosing and acting elements which go to make up controlled behaviour in precise terms. We will define them as formal and analytical scanning of the environment, setting objectives, drawing up plans of what to do before we have to face a change and then implementing them. We will regularly check on progress and change our behaviour to keep on route to the objective.

But as soon as we recognise that feedback mechanisms have an additional behavioural choice, we will have to re-evaluate what we are doing. That choice is bounded instability in which specific paths of development are inherently unpredictable over the long term, but nevertheless display recognisably familiar, but irregular, patterns. The choice open to managers is then one of designing their actions to secure stability, or designing their actions to secure and cope with bounded instability. Where success requires innovative and creative interaction with other organisations and people who constitute the environment, the choice has to be that of bounded instability. It is in this state that feedback systems are capable of continuing creativity. Where an organisation is not required to be innovative, but is required simply to adapt to a given environment, to keep doing the same thing until an environment over which it has no influence requires otherwise, then the appropriate choice is that of stability. Success in today's business world clearly requires the bounded instability choice.

Planning for the short term and for project execution

When managers think in terms of acting to secure and cope with bounded instability, they will recognise that they face a spectrum of change situations. Over the short term the consequences of changes created by and impacting upon the system are to some useful extent predictable. The change situation is closed and contained. In these situations all the conditions required to be able to control the business in a planned or ideological manner are met. When they recognise the dynamic of success as chaotic, managers will place even more emphasis on tight, short interval control. They will do this because it provides an important element of stability to a business that has to operate in conditions where the long-term future is unknowable. They will emphasise short interval control because it automates responses to short-term consequences of change, leaving time to attend to changes having longer term, unknowable consequences. They will emphasise short interval control because such a control system provides the means consistently to deliver low cost, high quality and appropriate service levels.

When managers come to execute a specific long-term project, the sequences of actions required to carry it out are usually predictable. Project execution can then be controlled in a planned manner, even though its long-term financial outcome may not be capable of being planned.

Simultaneous planning and complex learning

But managers who recognise the nature of bounded instability will also design actions to deal with the open-ended nature of change over the long term. They will recognise that open-ended change removes all the conditions required for the practice of the planning and ideological modes of control and development. They will therefore abandon all attempts at long-term planning and envisioning as a comprehensive means of developing the business over the long term. They will rely instead on complex learning in groups to produce emergent intention, strategy, culture and business philosophy. They will accept the inevitable unpredictability and irregularity of the innovative, the creative and the new.

The advice to abandon long-term planning is not advice to abandon all concern with the long term. It is not advice to focus on short term and specific project control alone, to avoid taking risks and to run for cover by seeking to operate only in conditions which are closed or contained. The advice is to search for realistic modes of maintaining and coping with bounded instability and consequent open-ended change.

The art of management is the ability to alternate between very different forms of control at different points in time, to ensure that they are being applied simultaneously in different parts of the organisation. The advice is not to abandon concern with the long term, but to identify more effective frameworks within which to design actions to deal with the long term.

8

Participation, Hierarchy and Stability

The rational, planning approach to managing a business is built firmly on formal hierarchies of managers that are as simple and understandable as possible. The operation of hierarchical structures requires clear job definitions, allocating responsibility for tasks together with clear allocation of the authority and resource to carry them out. Power in the organisation takes the form of authority. That is, power is exercised and consented to according to rules, regulations and procedures. While the benefits of this approach are evident when changes are closed or contained, it is too rigid to cope effectively with open-ended change. This dissatisfaction with rigid hierarchy and power restricted by rules and regulations has led to many organisations prescribing the exact opposite. These prescriptions are to be found in the ideological approach to strategy formation.

According to the ideological view of the strategy formation process, an inspirational vision and a strongly shared business ideology, together with tight short-term financial controls, provide the stable framework within which managers are likely to undertake a high level of trial and error action. It is through this action, through learning from failed and successful actions, that managers incrementally adapt their business to its environment more rapidly than rival businesses and so achieve success.

What mechanisms are proposed to ensure that a high level of trial and error action does actually take place?

Given the high volume of random shocks impacting upon the business and the correspondingly high level of trial actions required to counteract them, any kind of central direction or control of the trial actions themselves is impossible. The business has to rely on people throughout the organisation undertaking trial actions within the common vision and ideology framework. This kind of behaviour is to be secured, according to the ideological model, in three ways:

- flexible organisational structures;

- loose job definitions and overlapping roles;

- more equal power distribution.

FLEXIBLE STRUCTURES AND THE EMPOWERMENT OF PEOPLE

Those espousing the ideological view of strategy formation differ on the organisational structure required to promote widespread participation in trial and error action. On the one hand, there are those who recommend a highly decentralised structure, held together by strong financial controls. The idea is that people working in small units close to the market-place, will be more able to identify and carry out appropriate trial actions. Coherence and consistency would then be maintained by the centre applying tight financial controls and fanatically defending core values and the vision. On the other hand there are those who point to the sacrifice in cross fertilisation and overall organisational synergy which is bound to follow from highly decentralised structures. Those taking this view espouse more complex matrix or network type structures as a means of bringing people together across functional and business unit boundaries and as a means of bringing experimental actions to the centre of the organisation. It is recognised that working in such structures is more difficult than in simpler decentralised ones, but this is seen to be outweighed by the benefits of cross fertilisation and the challenge which the more difficult structure brings with it. All agree on cutting out layers of middle managers to improve communication.

The second mechanism required to bring forth high levels of trial actions relates to appropriate role and job definitions. Here there is agreement on the part of those taking the ideological view. They propose overlapping roles and loose job definitions. Because the environment is so complex and rapidly changing, it is necessary for everyone in the organisation to take an interest in everything. Clear role and job definitions simply put people in boxes and cut down on the range of perceptions and thus actions. The advice is to tear up the rule books and free people to cope with the environment.

The third mechanism also has to do with creating greater freedom for action. To achieve a high level of trial action, people within the organisation must be empowered to act. What is proposed, therefore, is widespread participation in decision making and the dispersal of power throughout the organisation, including greater decentralised power to allocate resources.

The whole idea is to create the flexible organisation through structural means. There are at least three serious problems with this set of recommendations:

1. Short interval control and its requirements.
2. Garbage can decision making.
3. Organisational learning.

Short interval control and its requirements

Those espousing the ideological view recommend complex (and thus unclear) organisational structures, flat structures (and thus stretched management resources), loose job definitions (thus unclear hierarchies), as well as widely distributed power to allocate resources. They couple this advice with the need for tight short-term financial control as the means, together with vision and ideology, of keeping the whole control system stable. It is recognised that this is a paradox summed up in the phrase 'loose-tight' control.

However, when one considers what is necessary for the operation of an effective short interval control system, it becomes clear that the advice is not a paradox, it is a direct confusion. The essence of tight short interval control is the clear allocation of responsibility for carrying out predetermined tasks having reasonably predictable results to which rewards are tied. We cannot allocate clear responsibility for predetermined tasks unless those tasks are clearly defined. Loose role and job definitions accompanied by unclear hierarchies and organisational structures are completely incompatible with tight short interval control. Tight short interval control is essentially management by rules and manuals. Tearing them up simply destroys the system. The operation of an effective short interval control system also requires management resource. The essence of this form of control is frequent and regular formal review and reporting. This requires resources to collect and present information, to attend review meetings and promptly carry out corrective action. If the stripping out of layers of middle managers is carried too far, it will damage the ability to carry out tight short interval control.

Widespread participation in decision making and the dispersal of power to allocate resources are also incompatible with the practice of tight short interval control. The whole system is essentially a top down one in which top management sets targets, after some negotiation with those lower down, and then retains the power to allocate resources. It is through power to allocate resources that the top maintains short-term control and stability. Furthermore the point of distributing power to allocate resources, according to the model, is to empower people to take action to deal with that which has not been foreseen. The essence of short interval control is to delegate power to use resources in predictable circumstances for predetermined purposes. Allocating power to use resources in unforeseen circumstance would undermine the whole system.

Flexible structures and tight short interval control are thus incompatible and the choice is an 'either/or' one. It could well be worth sacrificing some level of short interval control effectiveness if that led to better strategy formation. But does it?

Garbage can decision making

On the face of it, widespread participation and much more equally shared power should lead to more people detecting changes occurring in the environment and taking trial actions to deal with the uncertainty those changes provoke. However some interesting studies have been carried out on the decision making process in organisations that do have flexible structures of the kind the ideological proponents put forward.

Universities and some state bodies have flat, complex matrix structures; unclear hierarchies; very loose job definitions; widespread participation in decision making; and a fairly equal distribution of power.

The studies have found that the decision making process in these circumstances takes what has been called a 'garbage can' form. Because of the very flexible structure, large numbers of people can concern themselves with just about any issue, which they can raise at just about any decision making forum. Decision making forums then take the form of a 'garbage can' into which issues, problems and solutions tend to be thrown in a somewhat haphazard manner. Added to this, the participation of people at decision making occasions tends to be fluid with different people attending at different times – there are few rules requiring regular attendance. What is attended to and how it is resolved depends upon who is present, how interested they are in the issue, what other issues are attracting their attention, what other work pressures are distracting them. In these circumstances, decisions simply emerge by pure chance. Equal power means *no one* has enough power to do anything.

The universities and other bodies surveyed in these studies do differ in important respects from the framework proposed by ideological theorists for businesses. First, universities tend not to have much in the way of overall visions, nor do they have very strongly shared cultures. One tends to find a few widely shared norms on academic freedom and fairness, but apart from that there are many different cultures according to discipline and faculty. Furthermore, the tasks carried out at universities have what might be called an uncertain technology. For example, it is not at all clear what constitutes good teaching. The experts carrying out the tasks, therefore, have to be allowed a considerable level of personal freedom of judgement. The result of this combination of flexible structure, lack of vision and shared culture accompanied by uncertain task technology is that very little in the way of organisational strategy gets formed.

> Unconnected strategies tend to proliferate in organizations of experts reflecting the complexity of the environments they face and the resulting need for considerable control by the experts over their own work, providing freedom not only from administrators but from their own peers as well. Thus, many hospitals and universities appear to be little more than collections of personal strategies, with hardly any discernible central vision or umbrella, let alone plan, linking them together. Each expert pursues his or her own strategies – method of patient care, subject of research, style of teaching.[2]

Now while the situation described above is no doubt appropriate for universities and hospitals, it is clearly not so for business enterprises.

There is, then, some evidence which suggests that flexible structures run a great risk of making strategy formation worse rather than better. The ideological approach places tremendous reliance on belief in visions and values to prevent this happening.

But there is further evidence that flexible structures and widely dispersed power do not deliver good strategy.

Organisational learning

The whole point of flexible structures and dispersed power is to enable those below the top level in the management hierarchy to detect and take action to deal with the large number of changes affecting an organisation operating in a turbulent environment. The whole point is to enable the organisation to learn about its environment and so adapt to that environment faster than rivals do. Flexible structures and dispersed power are supposed to improve the ability of the organisation to learn. But there are studies which show that widening participation and empowering people is no guarantee at all that organisational learning will improve.[3]

What these studies have found is that there is a very widespread tendency for people to approach learning tasks in group contexts in a manner conditioned by a particular mental model. People simply apply the assumptions which constitute this model without ever questioning those assumptions. The first assumption we normally make when we deal with an issue in a group context is that we are there to achieve a purpose as we see that purpose. The second assumption is that having formed a view on what should be done, we should operate to win and not lose. Our proposed action should carry the day. Third, we assume that we can achieve this by avoiding saying or doing anything that will provoke negative feelings, and thus strong opposition, from those with a different view of what should be done. And finally we assume that we should all be rational and avoid any emotional display as far as possible. Because we make these assumptions we then seek to manage the occasion, to own and control the task and to unilaterally protect ourselves and the others involved. Since each of us is doing this, we see each other as being defensive. We make assumptions about the motives of the others, but we never expose those assumptions to them. We make matters impossible to discuss and we pretend that we are not doing so. We become defensive and cover up our errors. The result is polarization of issues and games of deception, with very little real learning.

If we wish to learn new things in highly uncertain situations then we need to approach that learning task from a different perspective, one which we all find very difficult to do. We have to approach the task with open, questioning minds, rather than seeking to win. We have to surface threatening issues and expose the assumptions we are making for testing by others. This can be personally risky and threatening and hence we automatically avoid doing it. It takes a great deal of effort and it is very easy to slip back into the situation where we conceal things and seek to win rather than learn.

Since this mental learning model, automatically used by all of us, is the win/lose, concealing one, it makes no difference if we open up participation in that learning process to larger numbers of people. We will simply have many people performing ineffective learning tasks rather than a few. The real need is to improve the learning process and widening participation has no effect on this. Again universities provide an example. Participation at most meetings in these institutions is very much more open than it is in businesses. And the win/lose dynamics are far more, rather than less, prominent.

So, flexible structures and dispersed power can lead to decision making processes in which the sequence of choices depends entirely on chance – they do not lead to improved processes of learning; they lead to potentially explosive instability. The ideological model of strategy formation then has to rely entirely on belief in visions and core values to sustain stability.

FLEXIBLE STRUCTURES AND CHAOS

If a successful business is one in which the dynamic is chaotic, then it will be impossible for managers to form a vision of some future state to guide the actions of everyone in the organisation. It will also be necessary to promote many counter cultures in order to generate the different perceptions necessary for creative action. The forms of stability postulated in the ideological model will thus be absent. If in this situation we were to have flexible structures, widespread participation and much more equally distributed power, sequences of choices would be highly unstable. Chaos is bounded instability and we therefore have to look for the boundaries. These boundaries are provided by power which is unequal but distributed, and by structures and hierarchies which are clear. Where power is unequally distributed across managers with clear hierarchical roles, sequences of decisions will be prevented from shooting all over the place. Where power is highly concentrated, a very few can pursue a sequence of choices in one direction for a long time – or they can swing that sequence around in an erratic and highly unstable manner. Unequal power distribution provides the checks and balances which prevent this from happening. It provides the boundaries we are looking for in chaos as opposed to explosive instability. Different cultures also provide boundaries.

When we think in terms of bounded instability, rather than a polarisation between stability and explosive instability, we take a very different view of the role of structure, power and culture from that presented by the ideological model.

Having discussed the conditions which the ideological approach puts forward to enable trial and error action, we can now turn to the process through which such action is said to occur. The process identified is essentially a political one. Some change or galvanizing event provokes conflict on how it should be dealt with. Different options attract individuals or organisational sub-units who, in effect, become the champion of that option. The champion forms a coalition of others who have something to gain from that option, so building political support for its progression. The option chosen depends upon which coalition has the greater power. Politics and the use of power overcomes the initial conflict around options and once an option is chosen all work together to implement it.

Here, conflict may play a part in the selection of options to be considered, but the role of functional political activity is to resolve that conflict as quickly as possible, leading to consensus around the choice of an appropriate option for the organisation. The normal state for the organisation is consensus and commitment, and functional politics secures that consensus and commitment. It is a negative feedback, damping form of control which sustains cohesion and harmony. Any other form of politics is said to be dysfunctional. Successful organisations are politically stable.

If we approach organisational success from a bounded instability perspective, we take a different view of the role of politics in a business. We see it as an amplifying form of development, the purpose of which is to surface conflict and spread questioning attitudes. Functional politics then involves continual dialogue around contentious issues. It is the mechanism for attracting organisational attention to open-ended issues. Its function is to spread instability, within boundaries, necessary to shatter existing patterns of behaviour and perceptions so that the new may emerge. In continually innovating organisations, conflict, dissensus and lack of commitment will be the norm: it is only at critical points that periodic commitment and consensus around some particular issue may emerge. But that consensus soon dissipates around the next contentious issue. Political activity and the learning associated with it is essentially self-organising and it is the process through which the order of new strategic direction emerges. Politics is also a form of control. The need to secure and sustain enough political support to acting and using the company's resources ultimately constrains the behaviour of everyone in the organisation.

HOW CHAOS WILL LEAD MANAGERS TO THINK AND ACT IN A DIFFERENT WAY

Consider where the stable equilibrium mindset leads us. We observe that formal hierarchies with their rules and procedures establishing unequal but clear distributions of power and clear definitions of roles, do not work effectively when the organisation has to deal with open-ended changes and unknowable futures. So, we move to the opposite extreme and advise abandoning all these things in favour of flexible (and thus unclear) structures, overlapping roles and loose job definitions, and invitations to widespread participation through more equal power distribution. To prevent the organisation from disintegrating under these loose conditions we then insist on strong ideologies, strong beliefs in visions and values, to hold it all together.

However, the result of this extreme shift would be to destroy the short interval control system on which an organisation must rely when it handles the predictable. And the shift does nothing to provoke the development of new perspectives and complex learning processes required to handle the unknowable. More than this, the shift to an extreme position actually blocks complex learning because of the emphasis it places on ideology, that is, a suspension of people's critical faculties.

Adopting a dynamic systems perspective leads to a different response. Here the importance of hierarchy is recognised; unequal power and clear role definitions in the short interval control of the business. When it comes to managing the unknowable, clear hierarchies and role definitions, together with unequally distributed power are seen to provide the constraints, or boundaries, within which choices are to be made in unstable conditions. The processes required to handle the unknowable are self-organising ones. But they are self-organising in the sense of learning and building political support within unequal power and counter culture boundaries, not self-managing in the sense of everyone participating in everything.

The dynamic systems perspective is one that recognises the importance of contradiction and creative tension – that between clear cut rigid forms of control to handle the knowable, operating simultaneously with self-organising forms of control to handle the unknowable. This creates tension because these different forms of control call for different forms of behaviour, alternately by the same people, simultaneously by different groups of people. The choice is not 'either/or'. The choice is 'and/both'.

REFERENCES

1. Peters, T (1985) *Thriving on Chaos*, Macmillan, London.

2. Mintzberg, H & Waters, J A, see reference in Chapter 6.

3. Argyris, C *Organizational Defenses*, see references in Chapter 5.

9

Steps to the Learning Organisation and Emerging Strategies

To succeed in today's market conditions, a business has to be continually creative and innovative. Its managers need to be skilled in handling ambiguous issues, surfacing contention and generating new perspectives. Creativity is exploiting small changes to develop self-reinforcing virtuous circles. It is consciously managing the unknowable, positively creating conditions of bounded instability and relying on self-organising processes from which the unpredictable new may emerge. It means accepting that the future is unknowable, making it impossible by definition to have visions of future states or intentionally control outcomes.

It is noticeable that companies which in all respects are stable, simply carry on doing the same thing until they are overcome by more imaginative rivals. Companies which in all respects are unstable soon disintegrate. The nature of the border area between stability and explosive instability, the bounded instability of chaos, provides managers with a new scientific framework within which to understand the dynamic of business success. It provides a more useful mental model to design realistic actions in today's business world.

When the dynamics of the business are chaotic, managers face a spectrum of change situations. At one extreme of that spectrum there is closed change where the short-term consequences of events and actions are predictable. At the other extreme there is open-ended change in which the long-term consequences of events and actions are inherently unpredictable. To succeed, managers have to control and develop the business in all change situations. But the form of control and development they have to use is dictated by the nature of the change situation. Short-term predictability makes it both possible and essential to apply planning forms of control and development to that short term. But because the long term is completely unknowable in specific terms, managers have to adopt a form of control and development that enables new strategic direction to emerge through a process of self-organising political interaction and real time learning.

The recognition of chaotic dynamics, and the restricted short-term role to which planning has consequently to be relegated, does not amount to advice to ignore the long term. Instead it points to a far more realistic recognition of the essentially ambiguous and uncertain nature of that long term. It points to:

- the nature of those creative learning activities required to deal effectively with that ambiguity and uncertainty;

- the need simultaneously to apply totally different forms of control and development, if a business is to succeed;

- the creative tension and instability this need generates.

This chapter sets out what managers need to do in order to cope with both closed/contained and open-ended change situations. Consider first what is required to control and develop a business in open-ended situations.

ENABLING THE EMERGENCE OF NEW STRATEGIC DIRECTION

When the dynamic is chaotic, long-term consequences of events and actions are completely unknowable in specific terms, therefore managers cannot design actions to produce organisationally intended strategic outcomes. Instead, control has to be concerned with creating the conditions within which new strategic direction may emerge. That strategic direction will emerge partly as a result of the creative actions of managers themselves, partly as a result of the responses this provokes from rivals, customers, suppliers and regulators, and partly as a result of chance. Control is enabling, not directing, in conditions of open-ended change. Securing a given outcome through directing forms of control is not possible.

So, top managers in large organisations face a choice. On the one hand they could choose to take a chance and enable the unpredictable emergence of new strategies. The process will be accompanied by conflict, disorder and inconsistency. A strategy may emerge or it may not. It may be a successful strategy or it may not be. The alternative open to top managers is this: they could ostensibly reduce the risks of conflict, disorder and inconsistency by applying directing forms of control in open-ended change situations. They could insist that all should adhere to the long-term plan, the vision and the same values. The result will be the predictable blocking of emergent new strategic direction and since the dynamic is chaotic neither the plan nor the vision is likely to be successfully realised either. It will simply be a matter of time before such an organisation succumbs to its rivals. What seems like the safer alternative turns out to be the most dangerous one, because it does not take account of the dynamics of the business game. Trying to manage the outcome in open-ended situations carries with it the certainty of ultimate failure, while trying to enable the emergence of new strategic direction carries at least the possibility of success.

It is relatively easy to set out lists of prescriptions for successful directing forms of control in closed and contained situations. It is a far more difficult matter to identify what to do to enable the emergence of new strategic direction in open-ended change. That greater difficulty follows from the very nature of open-ended change. Its present ambiguity and future unknowability, the anxiety and conflict it arouses in people, make it impossible to establish specific prescriptions on how to deal with a wide range of specific situations. But there are a number of steps managers can take to increase the possibility of emergent strategy. These are grouped under the following seven headings:

1. developing new top management perspectives on control;
2. designing the use of power;
3. establishing self-organising teams;
4. developing multiple cultures;
5. presenting challenges and taking risks;
6. improving group learning skills;
7. creating resource slack.

Each of these ways of enabling emergent strategy are discussed below.

Developing new top management perspectives on control

A standard response usually follows, when it is suggested to top management teams that creative strategies cannot be intentional in an organisation-wide, shared, predetermined sense; that such strategies have to emerge; and that the role of top management is therefore not to set the intention, but to enable the emergence of strategy by creating the conditions in which key groups of managers can discover new directions. The response is that such suggestions amount to the abdication of control and an open invitation to managers throughout the organisation to do whatever they like.

The concern is that if top managers abandon the setting of overall intention and guiding rules, this will lead to one of two consequences. Either newly freed managers will undertake enthusiastically high volumes of inconsistent and duplicated actions that expose the business to unacceptable levels of risk. Or, managers exposed to the uncertainty accompanying the absence of clear organisational intention will focus excessively on the short term and avoid strategic thought and action altogether. The conclusion drawn is that the top has to set the vision and establish a consistent framework within which other rungs of management will develop the specific strategic actions, if order and stability is to be sustained. The unquestioned assumptions are that order and stability are consistent with creativity and that lower levels of management are incapable of dealing responsibly with high levels of uncertainty.

This kind of response is evidence of a mental model of control that is out of touch with the realities of open-ended change. Open-ended change means that prior organisational intention cannot be established because the future is unknowable. Top managers who insist on doing this are then either restricting the discovery of emergent strategy to the activities of a very small number of people at the top of the organisation, or they are blocking it altogether. Restricting the emergence of new strategic direction to the efforts of a small number at the top can be successful where those people possess outstanding business ability and where they are dealing with a reasonably small organisation. For the great majority of corporations these conditions do not appear to apply. A mental model of control which is couched exclusively in terms of order, stability, consistency, comprehensiveness and harmony is therefore highly likely to be a serious obstacle to success.

Abandoning a mental model in which strategic control is seen as checking progress along a predetermined path to a prior intention, does not mean abandoning control. It means abandoning an inappropriate form of control and replacing it with a more appropriate one. It means abandoning the fantasy of stability for the reality of bounded instability. Establishing the conditions in which managers at different levels can create and discover emergent strategy does not necessarily amount to an invitation to people to do whatever they like, provided that there are boundary conditions. Clear hierarchies of managers in which power is, by definition, unequally distributed provides an important boundary condition. Managers will then not do whatever they like; they will know that they will need to build appropriate levels of support before they embark on any new direction. They will know that their proposals have to be legitimated, and resources allocated to carrying them out, according to the standard procedures in the organisation. In other words, the distribution of power and the operation of the political system of the organisation will perform control functions even where there is no prior intention or clear direction. When top managers see their business political system as one that provides an important form of control, they will be less concerned that everyone will be able to do what they like. Even a powerful chief executive has to secure political support if he or she wishes to carry out his or her proposals. A properly functioning political system performs the same function at all levels in the organisation.

The alternative argument that managers will abandon all concern with the strategic if they are given no clear intention from above, is also based on a restrictive mental model of control. The activity of learning in a group is itself a form of control. It is a self-organising, self-policing form of control in which the group itself discovers intention and exercises control. Different perspectives and different cultures provoke managers into thinking about open-ended issues, and they prevent a group of managers from all moving together in disastrous directions. They provide the boundaries around instability.

The need to secure enough consensus before managers can act is another boundary around instability. Given the pressures to conform, we should be more concerned with generating enough instability than we should be with securing the stability of shared beliefs.

The first essential step towards emergent strategy is changing the mental model of managers at the top. Without this, inappropriate forms of control will continue. When they come to see politics and group learning as forms of control that require no prior organisation-wide intention, then they will be able to let go. They will come to see that control can be exerted by operating on the boundaries, not the process itself or the outcome. They will come to see the benefits of instability taking the form of inconsistency and pay the price of duplication.

Designing the use of power

We are all perfectly accustomed to the idea that the strategic direction of local communities, nation states and international communities is developed and controlled through the operation of political systems. We describe a system as political when a sequence of choices and actions is produced by the application and exercise of power. The political process is one of identifying issues and building support that is powerful enough to result in the enactment of particular choices around the identified issues. A sequence of choices and actions will only continue in a particular direction while those espousing that direction continue to enjoy sufficient support. That support is sustained by exercising power either as force of some sort, or as authority according to the rules and regulations of the system, or as influence expressed through persuasion and negotiation. Attracting attention for issues, building and sustaining support, occurs largely behind the scenes, in informal ways as pursued by 'the men in grey suits' operating in 'smoke filled rooms'. But political systems also have more public faces, consisting of institutions and procedures by means of which choices and actions are legitimated and given public backing, and through which their consequences are accounted for.

Business organisations also have political systems in the same sense as that described above. Business political systems consist of the same mixture of largely informal processes through which issues are identified and support built to attend to them on the one hand, and more public bodies that legitimate choices and actions, allocate resources and account for consequences on the other. With regard to the informal aspects of the business political system, we find much the same formation of special interest groups, coalitions, factions and 'pressure' groups. It is here that the real political power is applied, the real support sustained and the real choices made. With regard to the public aspects of the business political system, we find much the same formal bodies, the board of directors and formal executive meetings, performing much the same function of legitimating the choices made more informally and accounting for the financial consequences of the enactment of those choices.

The curious thing is this. While most managers, when asked how nations develop and control policy, would immediately describe the political process, few do so when asked how companies develop and control strategic direction. Managers seem to dislike thinking of themselves as politicians and most seem to shy away from explicit examination of how they and their colleagues are using power. Perhaps the reason for this lies in a mental model of control in which strategic direction is developed directly out of prior organisational intention and controlled directly by monitoring outcomes against predetermined targets. The discovery of chaos requires managers to question this mental model. Chaos points to a model in which strategic direction emerges from a political process through which individual intentions may converge. In the political process, organisational intention is retrospective rather than prospective. Organisational intention is a consequence of how power was exerted. We come to see the political as a control system applicable to a business in just the same way as it is to a local community or a nation state.

As soon as we see strategic direction as the consequence of choices that emerge from a political process, we have to pay explicit attention to how we apply power. Effective strategic management depends upon how managers design their use of power – it does so because the manner in which power is used has a direct impact on the dynamics of group interaction. And group dynamics have a powerful effect on how managers in that group work together and what they learn. What they learn together determines the strategic choices they make and the actions they take. The distribution of power and the way in which it is used provide very important boundaries around the group learning process from which new strategic directions emerge. By managing those boundaries top management exerts control. But control here does not mean control over the learning process itself, over the sequences of choices made, or over the outcomes of those choices. Such control is impossible when the dynamic is chaotic – the learning process, the choices and the outcomes are all emergent. Instead, control takes an enabling form. By managing the boundary conditions to produce bounded instability, top management make it possible for real learning to occur. And such learning may produce unpredictable new strategic direction.

Power and group dynamics

The application of power in particular forms has fairly predictable consequences for group dynamics. Where power is applied as force and consented to out of fear, the group dynamic will be one of submission. Or where such power is not consented to, the group dynamic will be one of rebellion, either covert or overt. If an organisation faces a clear threat, then the use of power as force may well produce the required results. But where the organisation faces an ambiguous open-ended future, the application of force is disastrous. Groups in states of submission or rebellion are incapable of the complex learning which is the development of new perspectives and new mental models. Innovative new strategic directions are highly unlikely to emerge from such groups: all the energy will go into fighting and avoidance.

Power is applied as authority when that application is in accordance with the procedures and rules of the organisation and when it is consented to on that basis. The predictable group dynamic here is one in which members of the group suspend their critical faculties and accept instructions from those above them. The dynamic is one of dependence and conformity. This constitutes an appropriate use of power and a beneficial group dynamic when the organisation faces closed and contained change. Then, prior intention can be agreed and incorporated into the rules and procedures. Dependence upon and conformity with the instructions of authority will produce efficient behaviour. This is the form of power and the group dynamic required for short interval control. But when the situation is open-ended, this application of power and the dynamic it provokes is disastrous. Again, new strategic direction will not emerge from such conforming groups in which individuals have suspended their critical faculties.

The kind of group dynamic that is conducive to complex learning has the following characteristics:

- It is one in which highly competitive win/lose polarisation is absent.

- It is one of open questioning and public testing of views and assertions.

- It is one in which people use argument and conflict around issues to move towards periodic consensus and commitment around a particular issue. But it is not one in which that consensus and commitment is the norm; it cannot be if people are searching for new perspectives all the time.

- It is one that is not dominated by dependence on authority or expert figures. It is not one characterised by avoiding issues and seeking unilaterally to control.

The dynamic that provokes new perspectives and allows changing mental models, is one that alternates between conflict and consensus, between confusion and clarity. The dynamic has the characteristics of chaos and the principal boundaries around that instability are provided by the manner in which the most powerful use their power and the existence of counter cultures.

What use of power is likely to be consistent with the kind of group dynamic required to enable complex learning? It is likely to be one in which the most powerful alternate the form in which they use that power: sometimes withdrawing and allowing conflict; sometimes intervening with suggestions and influence; sometimes imposing authority or even force. When managers design their use of power in this way they are actually sustaining the instability required to provoke new perspectives. But that instability is bounded because there is authority, clear hierarchy and unequally distributed power. There is no recipe available to design the use of power in many different specific circumstances. The true skill of the enabling leader lies in the ability to design afresh the use of power appropriate to each specific situation – a question of experienced-based reflection and judgement.

Establishing self-organising teams

Innovation, creative new strategic direction, emerges from a group process in which intentions and choices are developed through essentially political and complex learning activities. The manner in which power is distributed and used provides boundaries around those political activities and creates the conditions within which complex learning may occur.

197

If power is highly concentrated and always applied as force or authority, we get a very stable organisation in which very little complex learning occurs – the boundary conditions are too tight. The organisation can then only deal with whatever open-ended change the most powerful notice and are capable of dealing with. Strategy is the result of the intention of the top executive and unless that executive is exceptionally talented, the organisation will fail to develop sufficiently creative new strategic directions to survive.

If power is widely distributed and hardly ever used as authority, we get conditions of organised anarchy in which there is also very little complex learning – the boundary conditions are too loose. The result is very little in the way of new strategic direction for the organisation as a whole. Instead we find fragmented individual strategies resulting from individual intentions which rarely converge because the group dynamics are those of continual conflict or avoidance.

If power is unequal, but distributed and applied in forms which alternate according to the circumstances, we find a flexible, fluctuating boundary around the political process that enables complex learning. But the important point is that establishing such a boundary does not ensure that such learning will occur or that it will produce some outcome that can be predetermined or guaranteed to be successful. The political and learning activity that may produce creative choices is spontaneous and self-organising. We cannot instruct anyone to have a creative idea in an open-ended situation. We cannot orchestrate factions and coalitions between people guaranteed to support the right idea, because when the situation is open-ended we cannot know what the right idea is. All we can do is control the boundaries within which behaviour favourable to the emergence of an innovative choice might occur. We have to leave the choice and the culture to the spontaneous self-organising ability of people in groups operating in favourable conditions.

Top management can, however, establish groups of key managers to operate in a spontaneous and self-organising manner. Workshops around issues or processes in general, or multi-discipline task forces set up to explore particular issues, are examples.

Freedom to operate

For a team of managers to be self-organising, it has to be free to operate as its members jointly choose, within the boundaries provided by their work together. This means that when they work together in this way, the normal hierarchy has to be suspended for most of the time. Members are there because of the contributions they have to make and the influence they can exert through those contributions and their own personalities. This suspension of the normal hierarchy can only take place if those on higher levels behave in a manner which indicates that they attach little importance to their position for the duration of the work of the group.

Discovering challenges

In addition, a team will only be self-organising if it discovers its own challenges, goals and objectives. This means that top managers setting up such a team must avoid the temptation to write terms of reference, set objectives or prod the group to reach some predetermined view. Top managers have to take the chance that their group may produce proposals of which it may not approve. Instead of terms of reference, targets and agendas, top management establishing a self-organising team will present it with some ambiguous challenge. There is no point in setting up such a group unless those at the top are genuinely looking for a new perspective. The ambiguous challenge may be to find a better organisational structure. Or it may simply be to identify strategic issues and choices the organisation should be attending to. Or it may be to produce proposals for a new product or promotional campaign. The task is to work at contradictions and anomalies.

Generating new perspectives

Since the purpose of setting up self-organising teams is to generate new perspectives, it is important to draw membership from a number of different functions, business units and hierarchical levels. Middle management is a much under-utilised resource in most companies when it comes to developing new strategic directions. These managers are closer to the action and more likely to be detecting contradictions, anomalies and changes from which new strategic direction is born. By drawing people from different levels and units, we widen perspectives and overcome the inherent inflexibility of existing structures and systems.

A self-organising group in the sense in which it is being used here is not just any group of people thrown together. The groups need to be designed. That design may be of a self-selecting kind when individuals select other individuals, on the basis of expected contribution, to form a faction or coalition around some issue. Alternatively, self-organising groups may be more formally designed where higher level managers select subordinates to form a group. This selection needs to be made on the basis of personality and likely contribution, not position in the formal hierarchy, and the effectiveness of such groups can be increased by formally tying performance appraisal to contribution to these teams.

Self-organising teams may be set up with many different focuses. There may be a strategy group for the organisation as a whole. This should not simply replicate the board or the formal top executive, but bring in other levels as well. Strategy groups may be formed for a particular business unit and function, but they should include people from other units and functions too. The purpose of these groups is to identify and discuss issues, not prepare plans or see visions. Task forces may be set up to develop specific projects. It is of great importance that these self-organising groups receive the interest and support of the institutionalised bodies of the organisation. There must be 'permission' to fail if self-organising groups are to function effectively.

The heart of strategic management lies in the strategic issue agenda of the business. The number and activity levels of self-organising teams has a direct bearing on this. Instead of shelving issues, innovative companies set up teams of middle managers to explore these issues. And they are not concerned at any duplication this may cause, or competition it may generate between teams. The costs of duplication and competition are more than offset by the different perspectives generated.

Developing multiple cultures

Open-ended change makes it impossible to establish prior organisational intention, either as vision or as long-term objective, and then ensure that actions throughout the organisation are consistent with that intention. Instead, top management has to enable the exercise of individual initiative and the development of convergent individual intentions through the continual building and progressing of strategic issue agendas. Top management can do this by adopting an appropriate mental model of control, one that recognises the importance of disorder, conflict and instability in the generation of the new perspectives upon which creative strategies depend. New perspectives are blocked when people strongly share the same culture. When people strongly share a culture, they are in effect using the same unconscious mental models to interpret what is going on around them and to design their responses to change. Since they all see the world in much the same way, they are unable to provoke each other to different insights. We usually see the organisational challenge and the difficulty as one of bringing about a common culture. In fact it is far more difficult to keep different cultures alive, because of the power of group conformity. Top management should therefore see its role as one of actively promoting, counter cultures in the organisation, rather than trying to change diverse cultures into one common one.

There are a number of ways in which management can develop counter cultures:

- Rotating people between functions and business units. The motive for doing this is usually one of developing wider experience in executives. It is usually seen as a method of management development, in which a cadre of managers with the same management philosophy is built up throughout the organisation. This tendency needs to be overcome by the design of development programmes that stress the importance of cultural diversity rather than uniformity.

- A more effective way of promoting counter cultures is that practised by Canon and Honda. Here managers are hired in significant numbers, mid-way through their careers in other organisations. The explicit intention is the establishment of sizable pockets of different cultures that conflict with the predominant culture. It is important that this should be done at different levels in the hierarchy, not confined to one or two top executives.

- The use of outsiders on some of the self-organising teams in the organisation.

Presenting challenges and taking risks

Active strategic issue agendas evolve out of the clash between different cultures in self-organising teams. Top management can provoke this activity by setting ambiguous challenges: instead of trying to set clear objectives, top management should throw out half formed issues for others to develop. Problems without objectives should be posed intentionally to provoke emotion and conflict leading to active search for new ways of doing things.

This activity of presenting challenges should also be a two way one. Top executives should hold themselves open to challenge from subordinates. General Electric has developed this into a regular process that it calls the 'work-out', in this case a business leader talking to a small group of employees drawn from all levels, outlining his or her views. The employees think about the ideas and about issues around their own jobs. They then reconvene to discuss the issues with the manager, who can accept or reject the ideas for improvement thrown up in the discussion, or can promise to think about them. If such a promise is made, the manager must report back to the group with a final decision within 30 days. This process is applied rigorously across the company, from top to bottom. It is structured so that managers cannot get away with doing nothing. Independent experts act as facilitators. They sit in on the sessions, make sure managers do not bully those who speak their minds, and check that they are sticking to their promises. The aim is to create an atmosphere where it is acceptable to speak out, where telling the truth is rewarded and where bosses who yell at people for speaking out are not.

Provoking challenges and holding oneself open to challenge involves taking bigger personal risks. But taking chances and enabling creative strategies to emerge are closely intertwined. And this applies not only at the personal level of the manager, but at the organisational level too. Some managers react to the idea that the future is unknowable and that the setting of prior organisational intention is impossible, by concluding that the organisation must avoid taking risks as much as possible. It should stick to the business it knows best and avoid uncertain long-term investments at all costs. The reaction amounts to saying, 'if you can't manage the outcome, don't do anything'.

Chaos forces us to confront the fact that no long-term outcomes can be managed, that all long-term outcomes depend upon chance to some extent. Managers who studiously avoid taking chances, therefore, face the certainty of stagnation and therefore the high probability of collapse in the long term. In business there is no sensible alternative to taking chances. Too rigorous an adherence to the 'stick to your knitting' principle will simply close off all possibility of developing creative new strategic directions. Managers who wish to develop creatively have to remain open to the possibility of the 'revolution', the radical departure from the existing business. For example, NEC's main business was the delivery of products and components with long life cycles made to the special specifications of Nippon Telegraph and Telephone Company.

> The new product development process began when a group from the Semiconductor and IC sales division conceived of an idea to sell Japan's first micro-computer kit, the TK-80, to promote the sales of semiconductor devices. Selling the TK-80 to the public at large was a radical departure from NEC's history of filling NTTC's routine orders. Unexpectedly, a wide variety of customers, ranging from high school students to professional computer enthusiasts, came to NEC's 'BIT-INN', a display service center in Akihabara. The continuing dialogues with these customers at 'BIT-INN' resulted in the eventual best-selling personal computer PC-8000.[1]

Running for cover simply because the future is unknowable, is in the long run the riskiest response of all. Instead companies need to expose themselves intentionally to the most challenging of situations. In his study of international companies, Michael Porter concludes that those who build sustainable competitive advantage on a global scale are those who intentionally position themselves to serve the world's most sophisticated and demanding customers. They intentionally seek the challenge of competing with the most imaginative and competent competitors. They make long-term investments in training and development, research and infrastructure without having any guarantee of specific returns from their investments. They encourage the development of clusters of effective suppliers.[2]

When managers employ a mental model that is built on the importance of feedback relationships and the long-term unpredictability such relationships generate, they do not run for cover. Instead they recognise the need to take chances without knowing what the outcome will be. They seek out challenging situations because they know that this is how to sustain the continual development of competitive advantage. This is how they learn.

The demand for consistency conflicts with the need to keep changing one's mind as the situation unfolds.

Improving group learning skills

New strategic directions emerge when groups of managers learn together in a complex sense. That learning is complex because it is not simply the absorption of existing bodies of knowledge, sets of techniques or existing recipes and prescriptions. It is complex because:

- it is the alteration of existing mental models of how things work, how we perceive what is going on, how we learn together and interact with each other.

- it is the development of new models with which to interpret continually new situations.

- it involves continual questioning of deeply held and difficult to surface beliefs.

- it can be threatening; it arouses anxiety and thus possibly bizarre group dynamics.

- it touches on deeply personal characteristics.

Given this complexity, group learning skills cannot be improved by taking neatly packaged courses to improve harmony and cohesion. Improving learning skills is a specific task for each group at frequent points in time. It requires surfacing the assumptions people are making and the ways they are behaving towards each other.

Since the emergence of creative new strategic direction in large corporations is so dependent upon this complex learning process, it is of great importance that key groups of managers should spend time exploring how they learn together. This is usually best done with some form of outside aid, facilitating managers' discovery of how they are affecting what happens in their particular group. Personality tests may be helpful here, provided that they are not used in a mechanistic way, but as a means of giving insight into why certain behaviour might be occurring.

The important point is that the kind of complex learning we are talking about is a self-organising process. It cannot be centrally organised. The role of top management in the strategic learning process is therefore an enabling and provoking one. It is necessary to create the opportunities for, and the atmosphere of openness in which, many small changes and different perspectives may be surfaced. The role of top management is to create the context and provide challenges. Creating the context means identifying and overcoming the obstacles to complex learning. These obstacles take the form of unconscious and thus unquestioned assumptions about how groups should learn together. These assumptions generate organisational defences, game playing and cover-ups. It is these that have to be surfaced and worked on. Obstacles to learning also take the form of managers focusing their concerns on their own position without perceiving how they interact within the whole system of which they are a part. Obstacles take the form of managers distancing themselves from responsibility for the way they are interacting and so blaming others or the system.

In practical terms these obstacles can only be overcome by managers in groups actually working on them. This will require a programme of frequent workshops. In his book, 'The Fifth Discipline', Peter Senge[3] recounts the story of the insurance company Hanover. Here a continuing, long-term programme was instituted for managers to work on their learning models and to expose their defensive routines. That company has consistently outperformed the industry averages for profitability.

Creating resource slack

Strategies emerge when the attitudes and behaviour of managers create a favourable atmosphere. They emerge when individual managers exercise initiative and intuition. They emerge through the hard work of learning together in self-organising groups, discussing and reflecting on what is going on and designing experimental actions to change the world they operate in. This creative work needed to deal with open-ended issues takes time and management resources. And investment in these resources has an unpredictable return. For lengthy periods it is quite possible that little will emerge from a great deal of discussion and experimentation. But without this investment in what appears to be management resource slack, new strategic directions will not emerge. A vital precondition for emergent strategy is thus investment in management resource to allow it to happen. This runs counter to the requirement for short term profit and short-term efficiency. But it is a price which has to be paid if new strategic directions are to emerge. The current fashion for cutting out layers of middle management, for reducing numbers of senior executives and loading them up with day-to-day duties can easily be taken so far that it destroys the ability of a company to attend to open-ended issues. Executives who work 12 or 14 hour days are unlikely to have the mental resources to attend to such issues. Therefore a careful judgement has to be made on the amount of management resource slack required to enable emergent strategy.

EMERGENT STRATEGY FOR THE LONG TERM

The dynamic systems perspective brings a coherent new view to the process of strategic control and development. It leads managers to abandon the idea that strategic direction can be controlled through setting prior, widely shared intention and monitoring outcomes. Instead strategic control is seen as control over the boundary conditions around the instability which is vital to the emergence of new strategic direction. Managers designing actions within this kind of mental model will seek to provoke the bounded instability of different cultures, conflict around issues and pressing challenge. Instead of focusing on consistency, order, the prevention of duplication, they will focus on contradiction, anomaly and ambiguity. They will understand the power of self-organising groups to create new order out of confusion.

Emergent strategy depends upon the functioning of the political system, the group dynamic, the impact of personality and the conditions in which groups can work at learning together. This requires intentionally creating bounded disorder and relying on self-organisation for the emergence of unpredictable, creative new strategic direction.

What is clear is that we cannot rely on structures and quantitative information systems, both inevitably inflexible, to enable emergent strategy. These are instruments appropriate for the other form of control to which we now turn.

PLANNING FOR THE SHORT TERM

Open-ended change is not the only change situation confronting a business. Consequently, control as a political learning process that enables emergent strategy is not the only control form required for success. Since the short-term consequences of events and actions are predictable in chaotic systems, managers are able to prepare in advance to deal with them. The day-to-day control over the existing business should therefore be based on clear, short-term organisational intention. It is control over outcomes secured through setting quantitative, time definite objectives, planning and monitoring. This requires clear hierarchies, clear organisational structures with precise job definitions.

The chaos perspective leads to the conclusion that organisational structures are largely irrelevant to the emergence of new strategic direction. We should not attempt to design structures or quantitative information systems with strategic considerations in mind, because such instruments of control are inevitably too rigid. For emergent strategy we have to rely on politics, learning – in short, on behaviour and informal group interaction. Organisation structures should, therefore, be designed to yield the most effective short interval control and to deliver competitive advantage to known market segments. The same applies to formal information and control systems. Once managers adopt this perspective they will only change organisational structures and formal information and control systems when an emerged strategy makes this necessary.

SIMULTANEOUS APPLICATION OF DIFFERENT CONTROL FORMS

The key point is that no business can choose to practise one control form rather than another if it wishes to survive. It has to practise short interval control using negative feedback through formal structures, systems and plans. It also has to practise amplifying feedback, the intentional creation of bounded instability to handle open-ended issues and enable emergent strategy. This depends upon politics, learning and behaviour. It is informal, spontaneous, self-organising and the outcome is unpredictable. A successful organisation practises both of these forms of control simultaneously.

This means that significant numbers of key managers have to be capable of alternating the way they work and behave. At some times they have to rely on analysis and the application of authority in formal situations; at other times they have to rely on their own personalities and influence in informal political settings. They have to use analogous reasoning and intuitive abilities; they have to challenge and be open to challenge. Above all they have to develop the ability to learn in complex, sometimes threatening ways with others.

The key message of dynamic systems models is that a preoccupation with order, stability and consistency in all time frames damages management creativity and the ability to cope with the unknowable. When the future is unknowable you cannot install techniques, procedures, structures or ideologies to control long-term outcomes. But you can manage the boundary conditions to push the organisation far-from-equilibrium where spontaneous self-organisation may occur. From that process, new strategic direction may emerge. Self-organisation is not formal or informal widespread participation throughout the organisation. It is not the same thing as self-managing teams. Self-organisation is based on peoples' judgements of each others' potential contributions. It is political interaction within the boundaries of unequal power and hierarchy. It is groups performing complex learning within the boundaries of different personalities and cultures.

The key question is not how to create stable equilibrium organisations, but how to establish sufficient constrained instability to provoke complex learning. It is through complex learning that businesses manage and create unknowable futures.

REFERENCES

1. Nonaka, I see reference in Chapter 4.

2. Porter, M (1990), *The Competitive Advantage of Nations*, Macmillan, London.

3. Senge, P see reference in Chapter 5.

Index